EASY PIANO

THE GIANT BOOK OF
CHRISTMAS
SHEET MUSIC

Arranged by
DAN COATES

W9-BWJ-097

Alfred

Produced by
Alfred Music
P.O. Box 10003
Van Nuys, CA 91410-0003
alfred.com

Printed in USA.

ISBN-10: 1-4706-1070-1
ISBN-13: 978-1-4706-1070-8

Piano keys: © Shutterstock.com / Ensuper • Brush stroke: © Shutterstock.com / foxie

Contents

Song	Page
All I Want for Christmas Is My Two Front Teeth	4
Angels We Have Heard On High	6
Auld Lang Syne	8
Away in a Manger	10
Believe (from *The Polar Express*)	12
Blue Christmas	16
Celebrate Me Home	19
The Christmas Waltz	28
Coventry Carol	24
Deck the Halls	26
Even Santa Fell in Love	31
Felíz Navidad	36
The First Noel	34
Frosty the Snowman	39
The Gift	42
God Rest Ye Merry, Gentlemen	46
Good King Wenceslas	48
Grandma Got Run Over by a Reindeer	50
Happy Xmas (War Is Over)	59
Hark! the Herald Angels Sing	53
Have Yourself a Merry Little Christmas	56
A Holly Jolly Christmas	64
(There's No Place Like) Home for the Holidays	80
I Saw Three Ships	66
I'll Be Home for Christmas	90
It Came Upon the Midnight Clear	68
It's the Most Wonderful Time of the Year	70
Jesu, Joy of Man's Desiring	74
Jingle Bell Rock	83
Jingle Bells	78

Jolly Old Saint Nicholas 86

Joy to the World 87

Let It Snow! Let It Snow! Let It Snow! 88

The Little Drummer Boy 93

Mele Kalikimaka 96

Nuttin' for Christmas 99

O Christmas Tree (O Tannenbaum) 102

O Come, All Ye Faithful 104

O Come, O Come Emmanuel 106

O Holy Night 108

O Little Town of Bethlehem 112

Pat-a-pan 120

Rockin' Around the Christmas Tree 121

Rudolph, the Red-Nosed Reindeer 114

Santa Baby 124

Santa Claus Is Comin' to Town 118

Silent Night 127

Sleigh Ride 130

These Are the Special Times 134

Toyland 138

The Twelve Days of Christmas 140

Ukrainian Bell Carol 144

Up on the Housetop 147

We Three Kings of Orient Are 152

We Wish You a Merry Christmas 148

What Child Is This? 150

When Christmas Comes to Town (from *The Polar Express*) 155

Winter Wonderland 162

You're a Mean One, Mr. Grinch (from *How the Grinch Stole Christmas*) 158

'Zat You, Santa Claus? 165

All I Want for Christmas
Is My Two Front Teeth

Words and Music by Don Gardner

Arr. Dan Coates

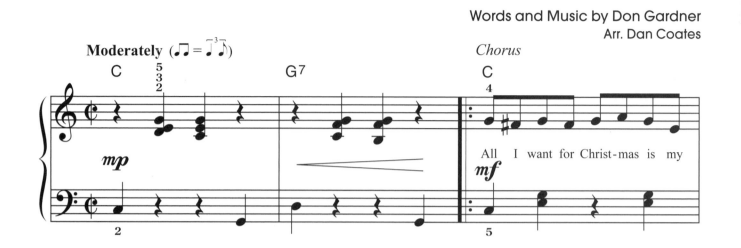

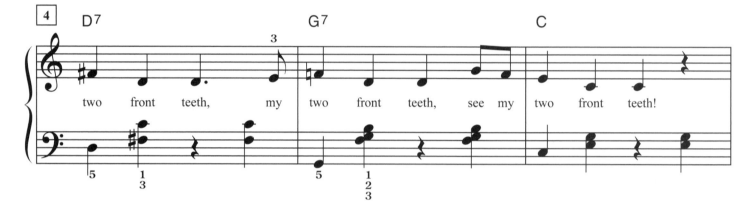

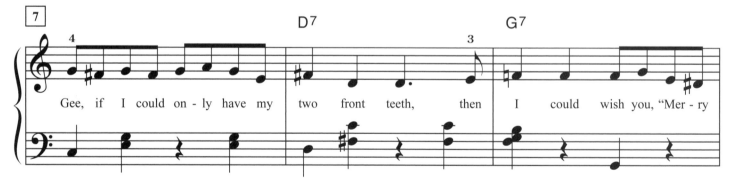

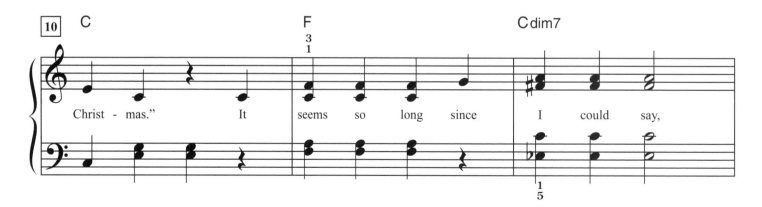

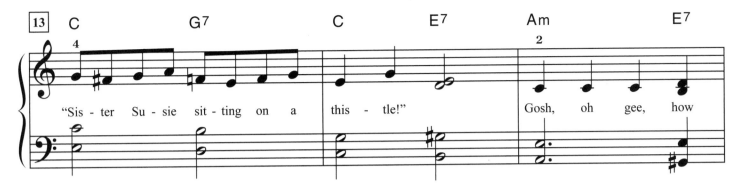

"Sis - ter Su - sie sit - ting on a this - tle!" Gosh, oh gee, how

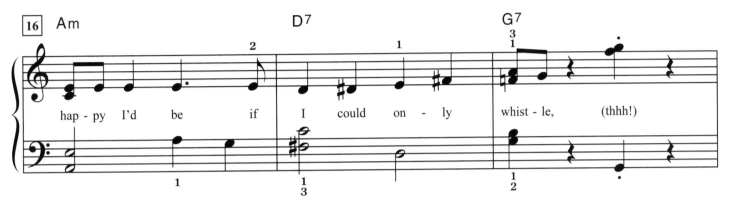

hap - py I'd be if I could on - ly whist - le, (thhh!)

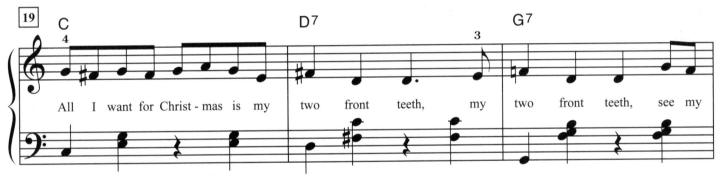

All I want for Christ - mas is my two front teeth, my two front teeth, see my

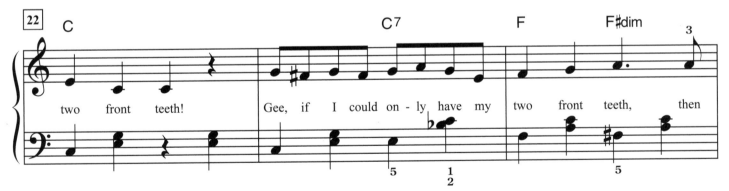

two front teeth! Gee, if I could on - ly have my two front teeth, then

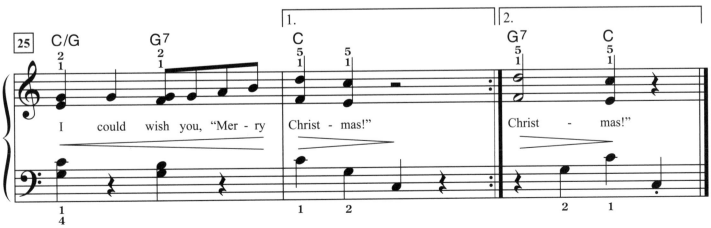

I could wish you, "Mer - ry Christ - mas!" Christ - mas!"

Angels We Have Heard On High

Traditional Christmas Carol
Arr. Dan Coates

Chorus:

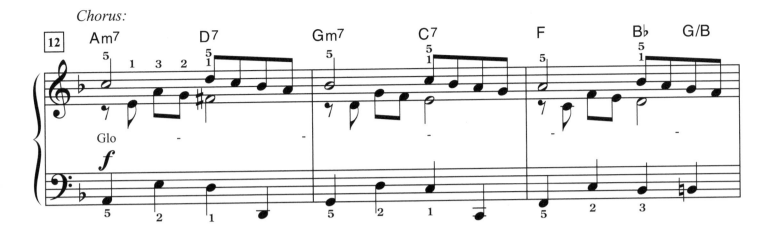

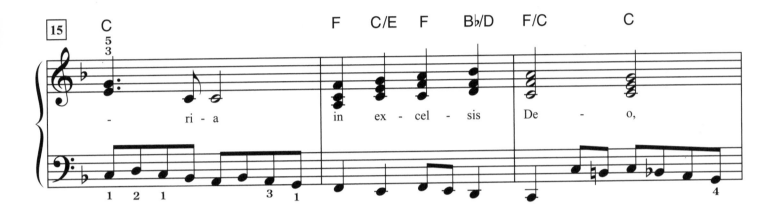

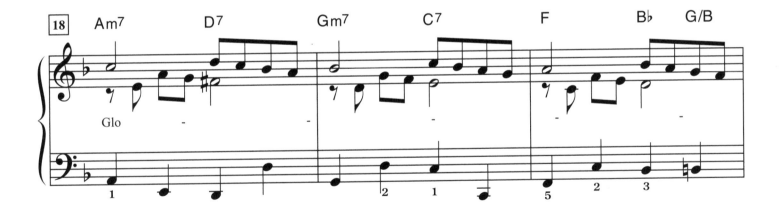

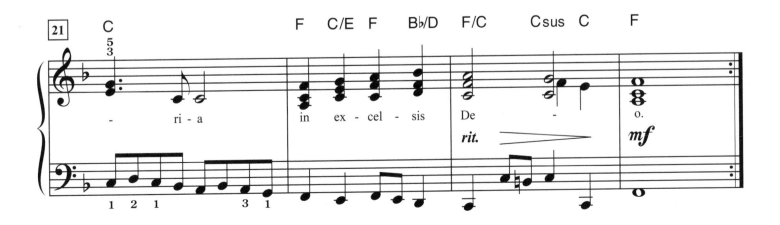

Auld Lang Syne

Traditional Scottish melody
Words by Robert Burns
Arr. Dan Coates

Moderately slow

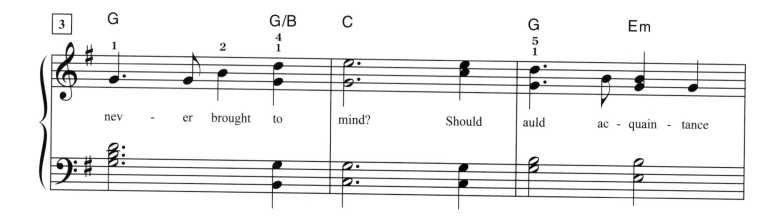

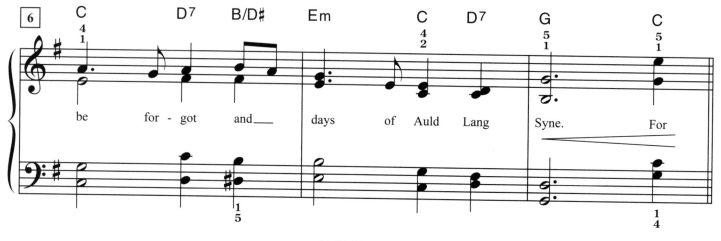

Chorus:

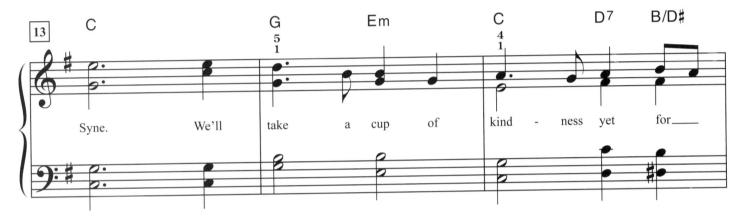

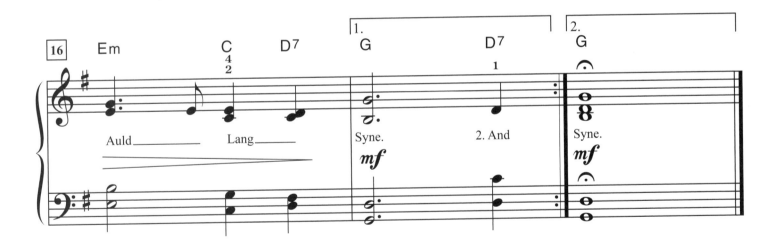

Verse 2:
And here's a hand, my trusty friend,
And give's a hand o' thine.
We'll make a cup of kindness yet
For Auld Lang Syne.
(To Chorus:)

Away in a Manger

Music by James R. Murray
Arr. Dan Coates

Slowly, with expression

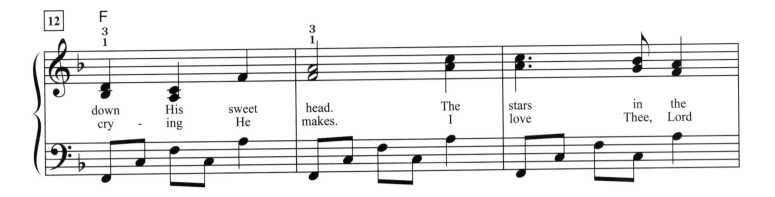

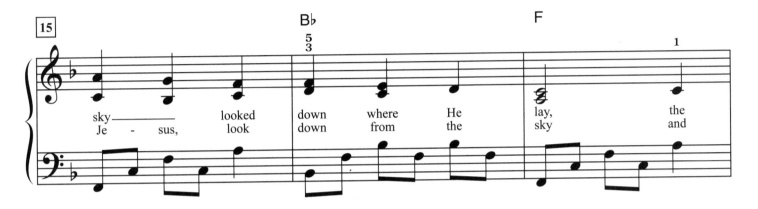

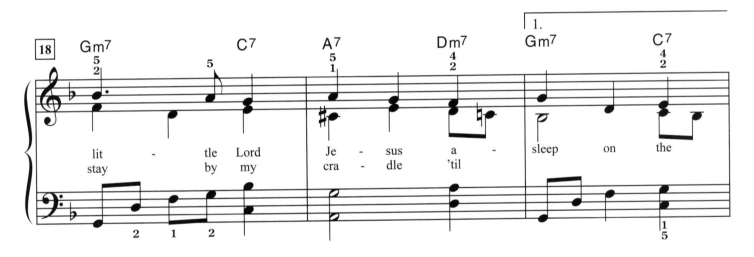

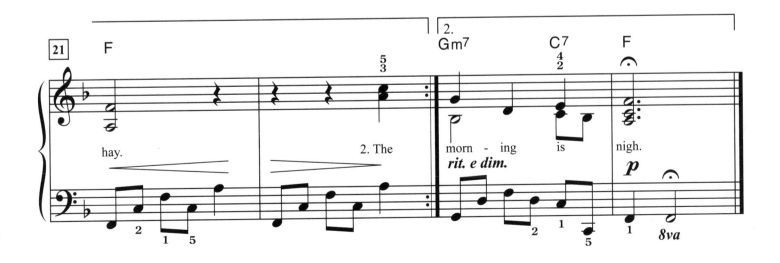

Believe

(from *The Polar Express*)

Words and Music by
Alan Silvestri and Glen Ballard
Arr. Dan Coates

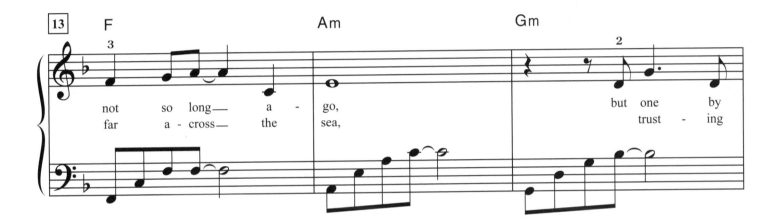

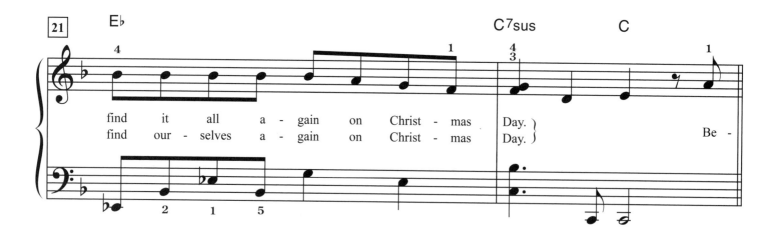

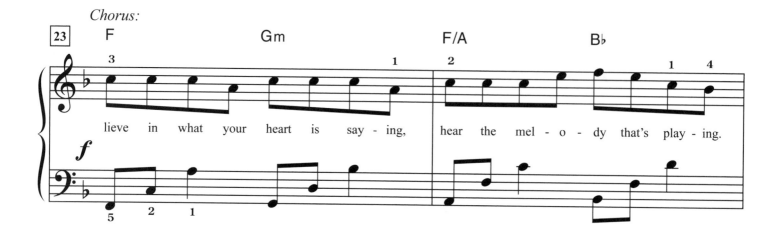

Chorus:

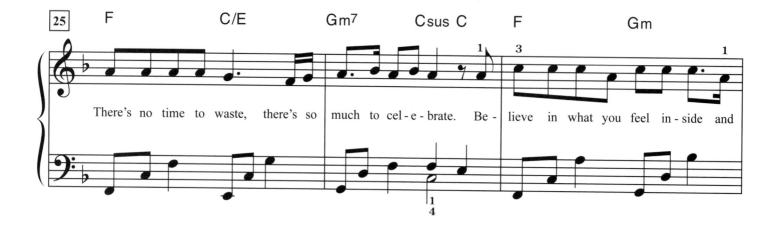

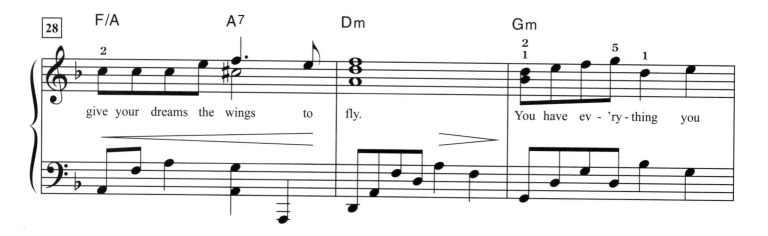

need if you just be - lieve.

lieve. If you just be - lieve,

if you just be - lieve.

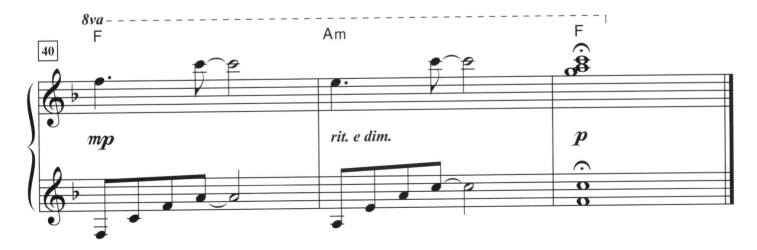

Blue Christmas

Words and Music by
Bill Hayes and Jay Johnson
Arr. Dan Coates

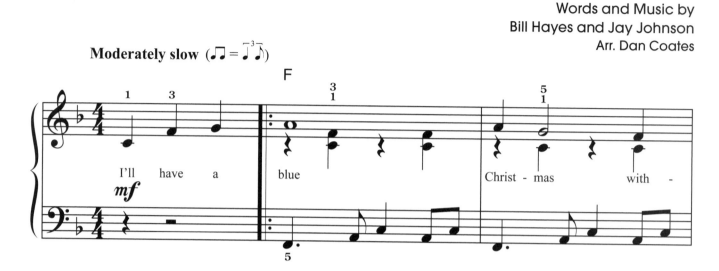

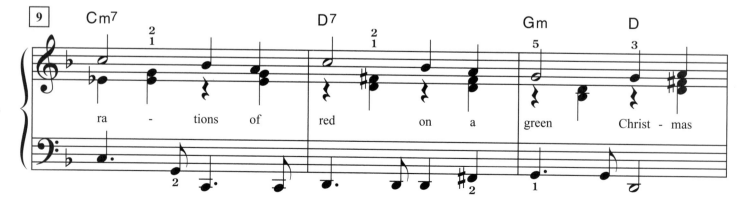

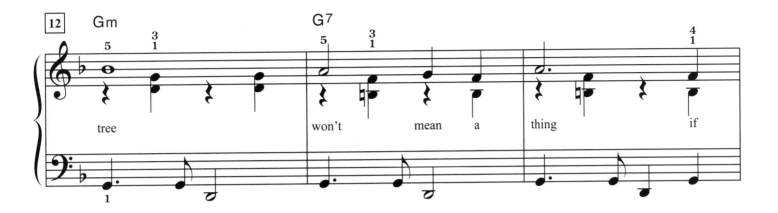

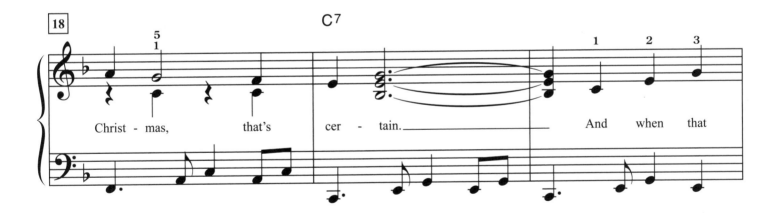

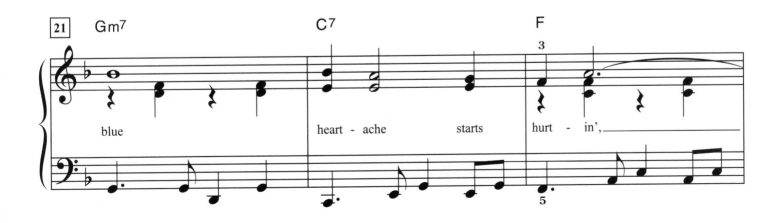

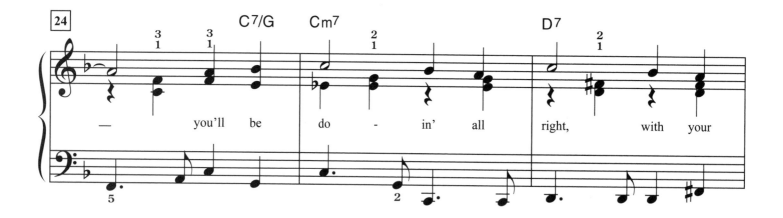

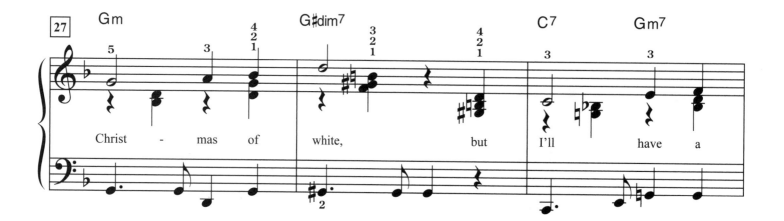

Celebrate Me Home

Lyrics by Kenny Loggins
Music by Kenny Loggins and Bob James
Arr. Dan Coates

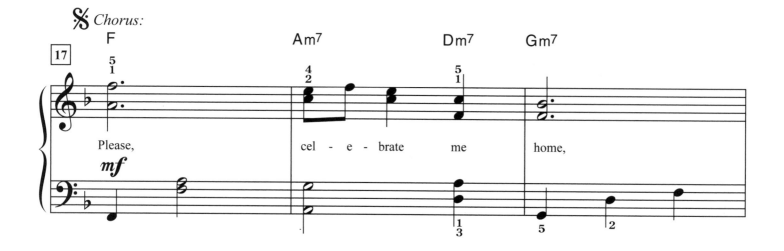

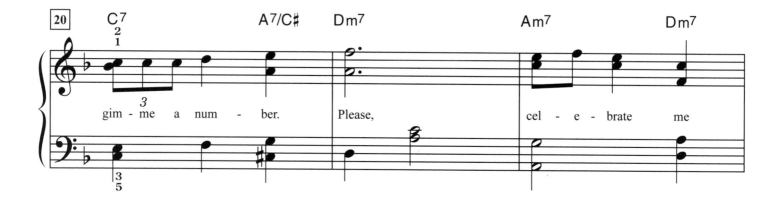

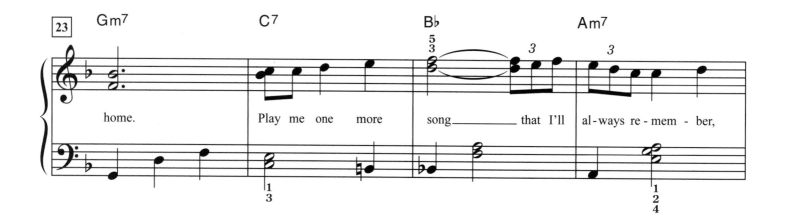

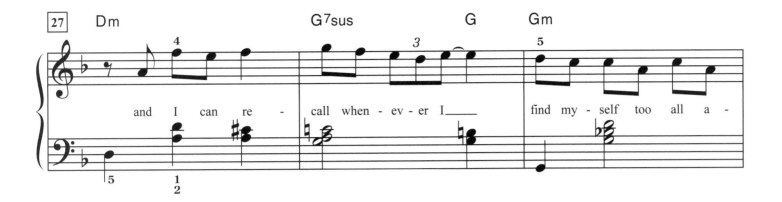

and I can re - call when - ev - er I____ find my - self too all a -

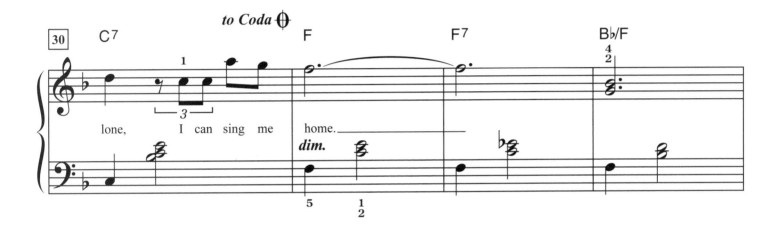

to Coda ⊕

lone, I can sing me home.____

dim.

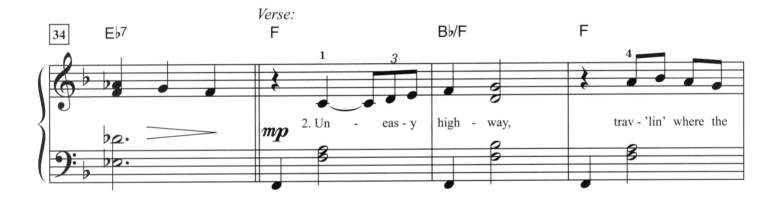

Verse:

2. Un - eas - y high - way, trav - 'lin' where the

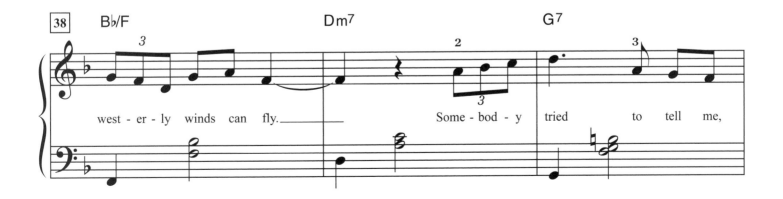

west - er - ly winds can fly.____ Some - bod - y tried to tell me,

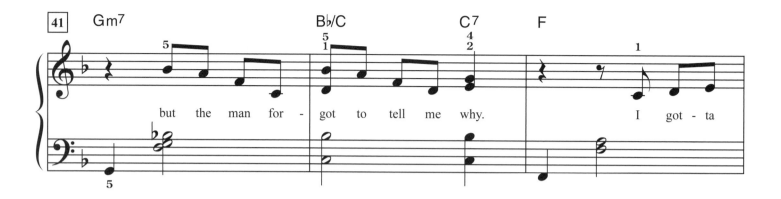

but the man for - got to tell me why. I got - ta

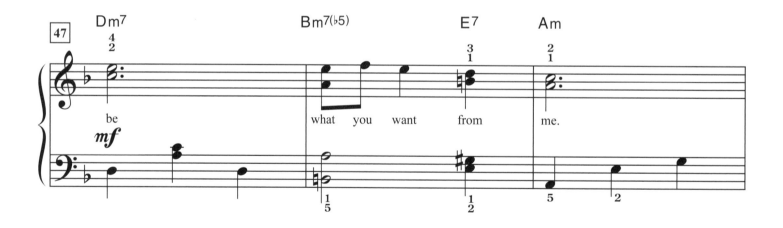

count on be - ing gone. *cresc.* Come on, ma - ma, come on, dad - dy,

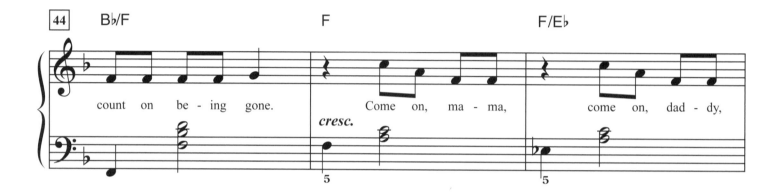

be what you want from me.

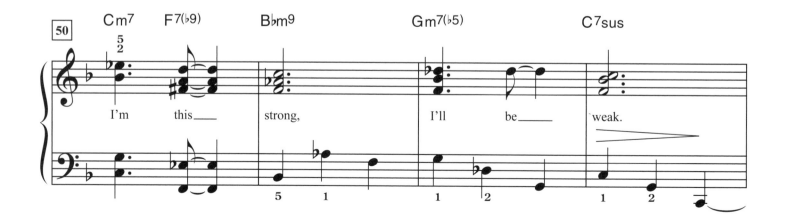

I'm this___ strong, I'll be___ weak.

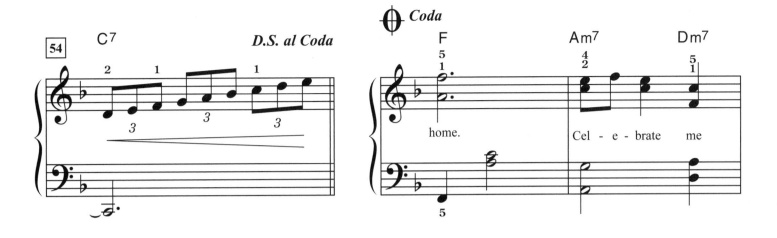

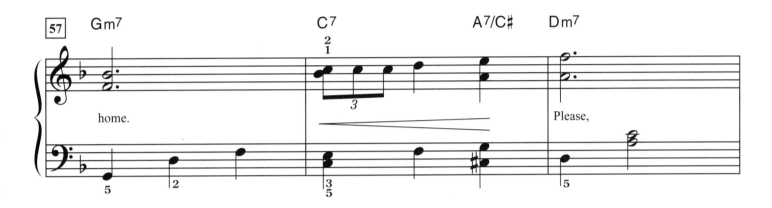

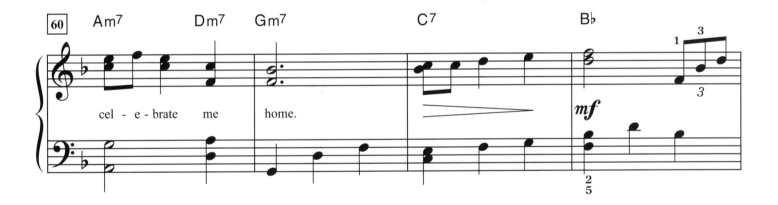

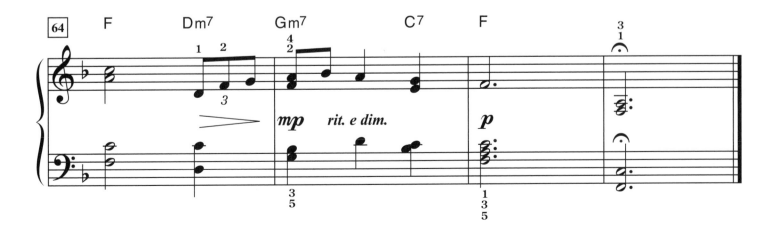

Coventry Carol

Traditional English carol
Arr. Dan Coates

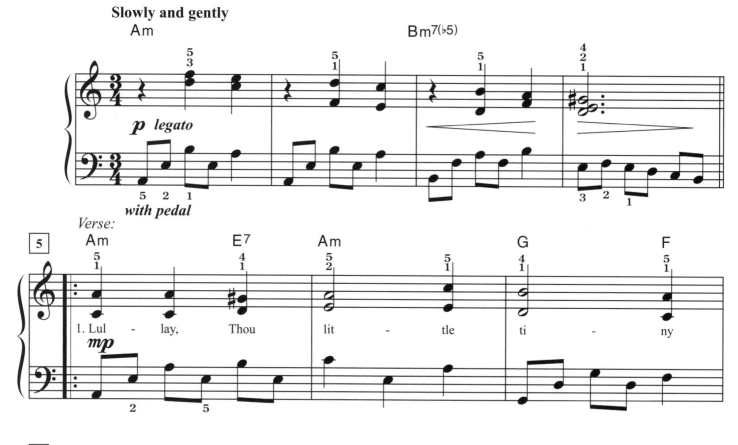

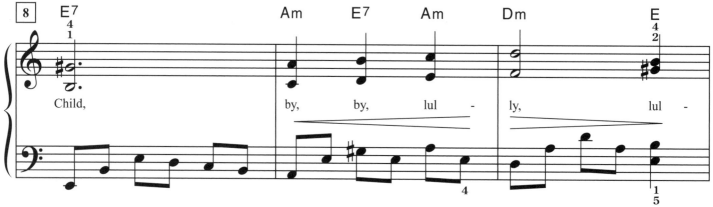

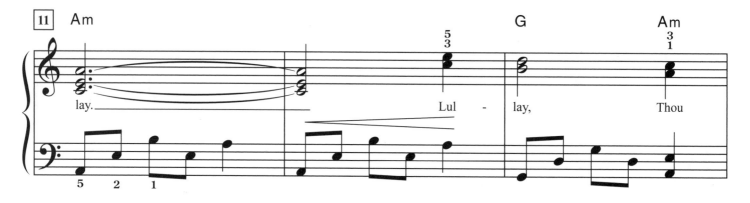

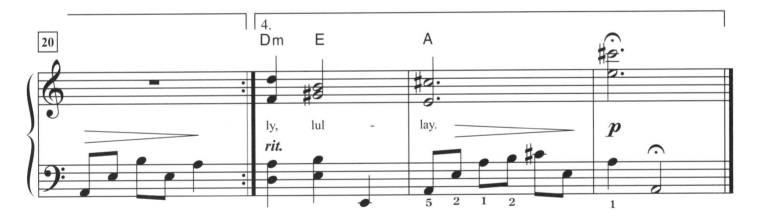

Verse 2:
O sisters, too, how may we do,
For to preserve this day
This poor youngling for whom we sing
By by, lully, lullay.

Verse 3:
Herod the king, in his raging,
Charged he hath this day
His men of might, in his own sight,
All children young to slay.

Verse 4:
Then woe is me, poor Child, for Thee!
And ever morn and day,
For Thy parting nor say nor sing,
By by, lully, lullay.

Deck the Halls

Traditional Welsh carol
Arr. Dan Coates

Brightly
Verse:

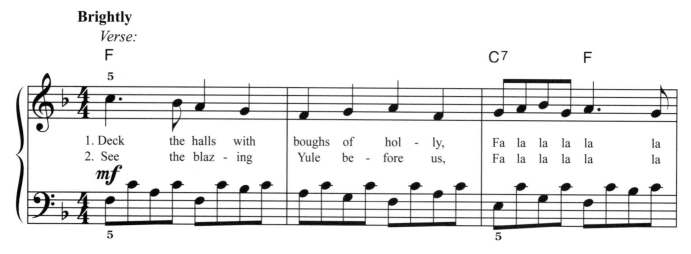

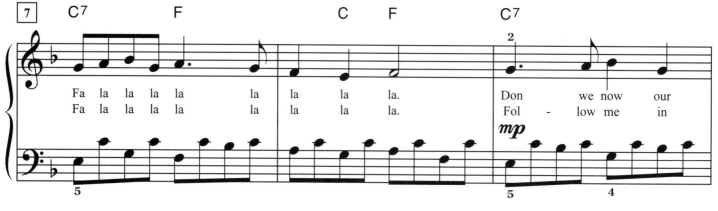

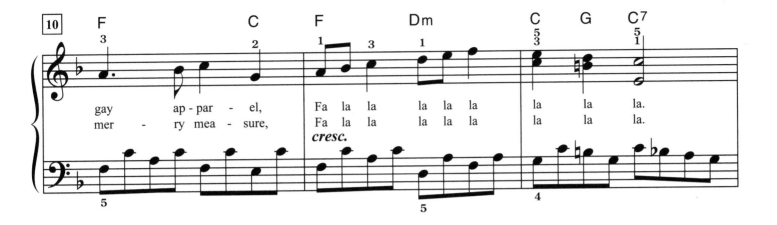

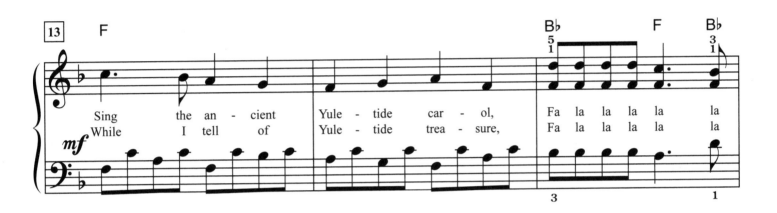

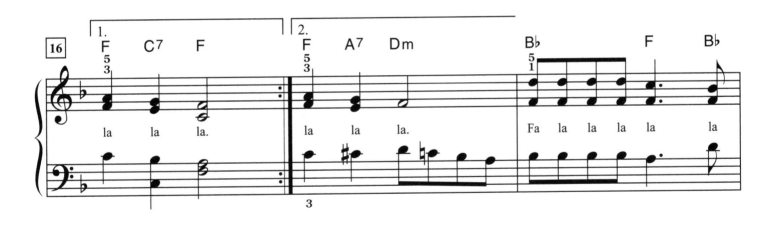

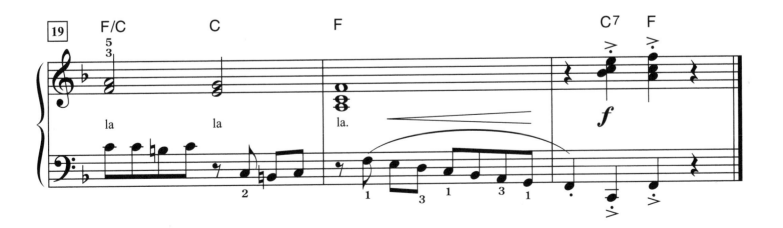

The Christmas Waltz

Words by Sammy Cahn
Music by Jule Styne
Arr. Dan Coates

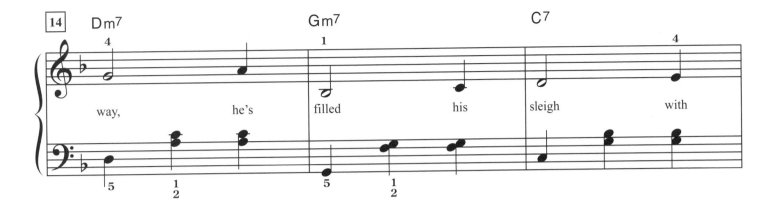

14 Dm7 ... Gm7 ... C7

way, he's filled his sleigh with

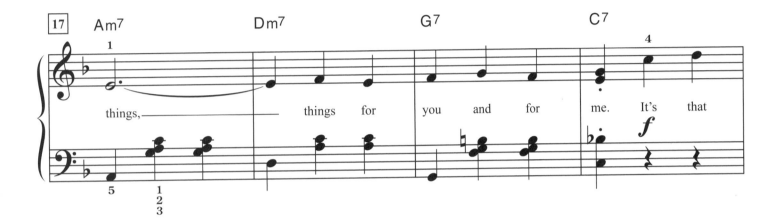

17 Am7 ... Dm7 ... G7 ... C7

things,_____ things for you and for me. It's that

f

21 F ... D7 ... Gm7

time of year,_____ when the world falls in

24 C7 ... F ... D7

love, ev - 'ry song you hear_____ seems to

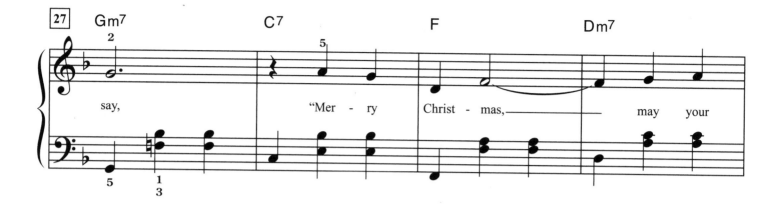

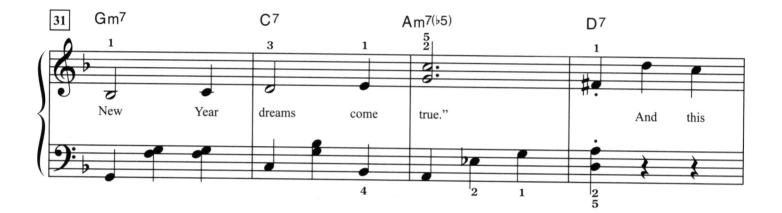

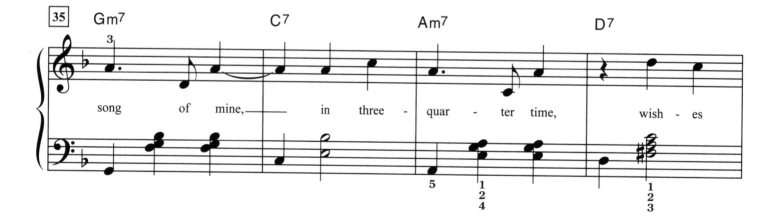

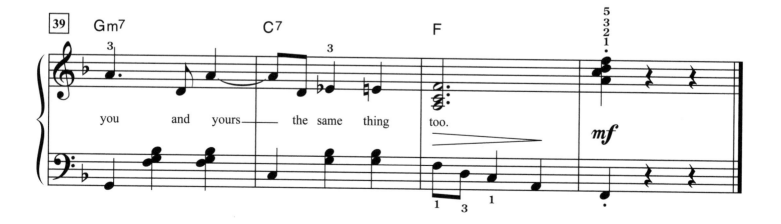

Even Santa Fell in Love

Words and Music by
Jim Brickman and Billy Mann
Arr. Dan Coates

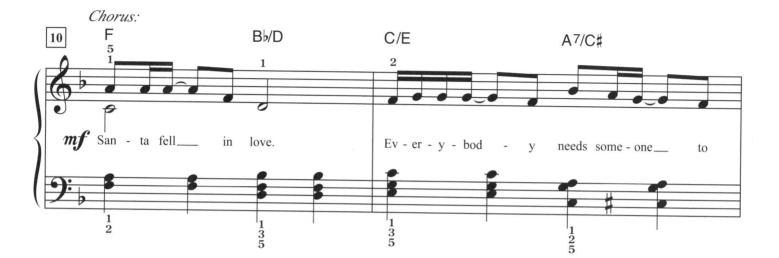

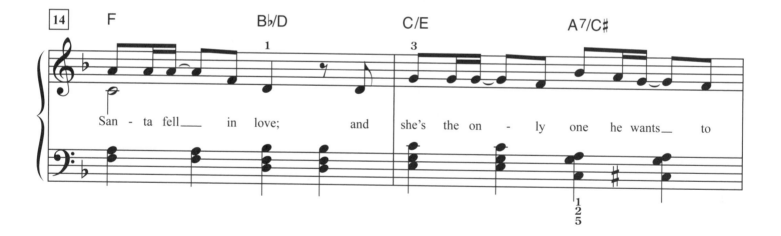

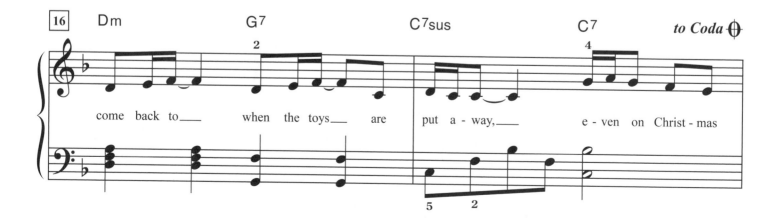

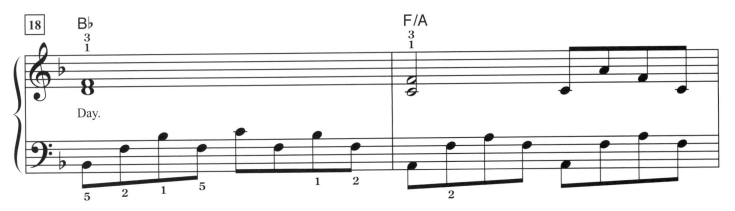

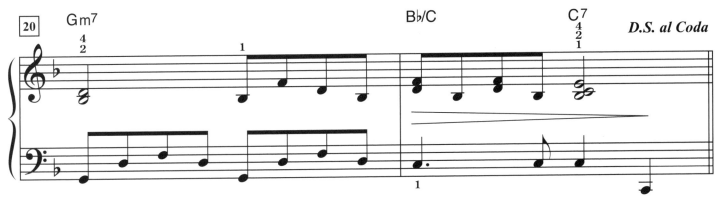

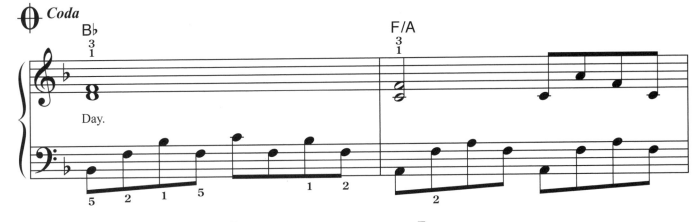

Verse 3:
She sees his eyes are all aglow,
Anticipating children laughing in the snow.
And with just his Christmas touch,
Under mistletoe, before the rush,
Mrs. Kringle feels the tingle in her heart.
(To Chorus:)

The First Noel

Traditional English carol
Arr. Dan Coates

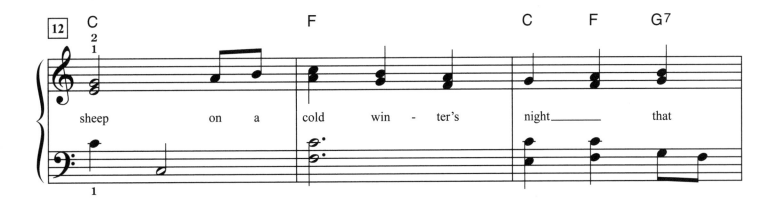

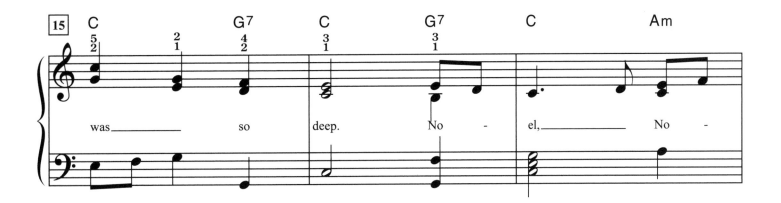

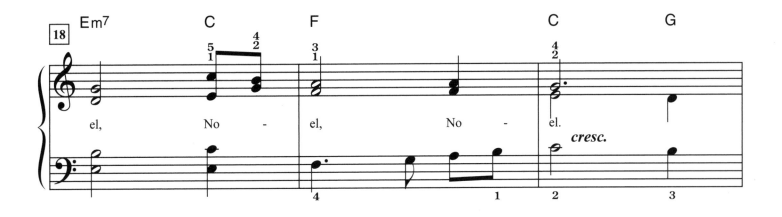

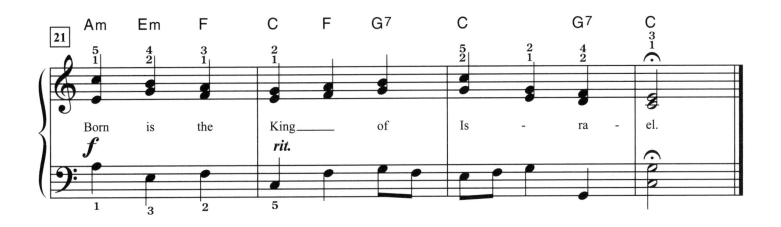

Felíz Navidad

Words and Music by José Feliciano
Arr. Dan Coates

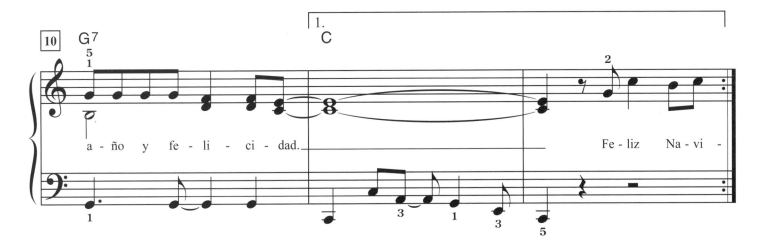

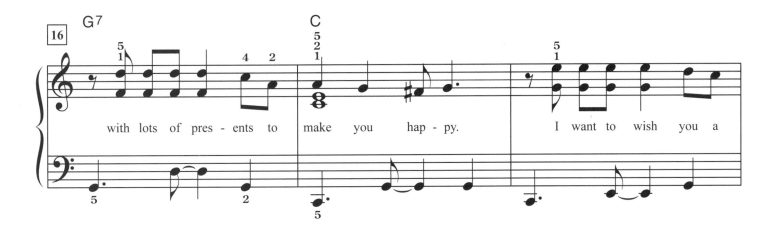

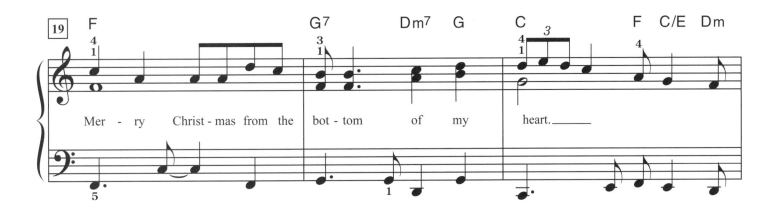

I want to wish you a Mer - ry Christ - mas, with mis - tle - toe and

lots of cheer. With lots of laugh - ter through - out the years from the

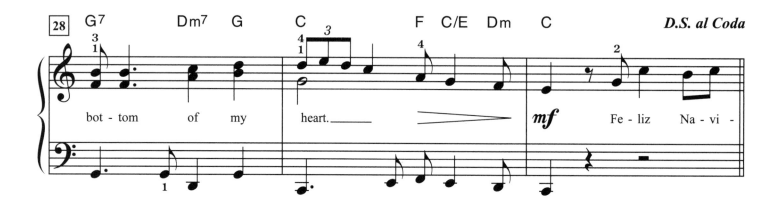

D.S. al Coda

bot - tom of my heart. *mf* Fe - liz Na - vi -

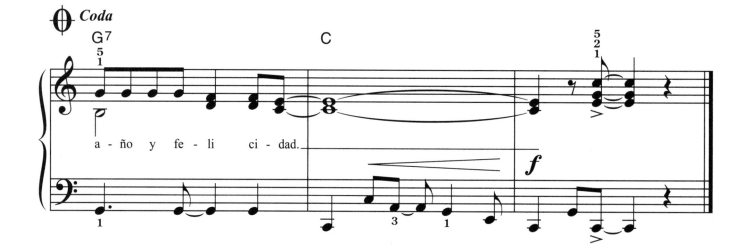

Coda

a - ño y fe - li - ci - dad. *f*

Frosty the Snowman

Words and Music by
Steve Nelson and Jack Rollins
Arr. Dan Coates

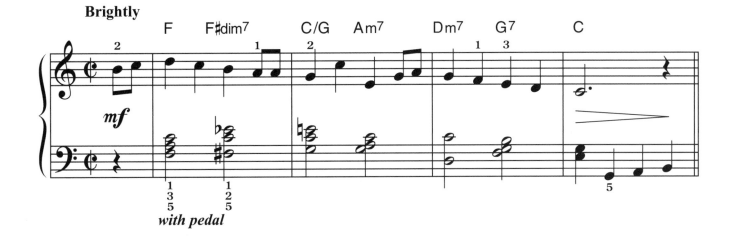

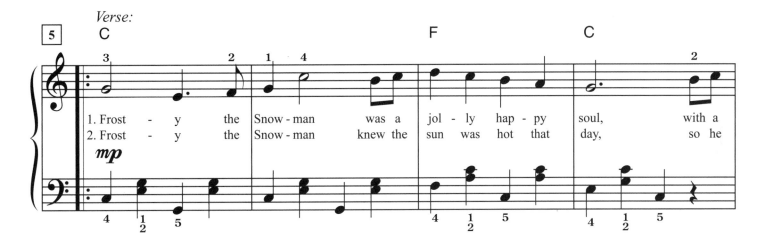

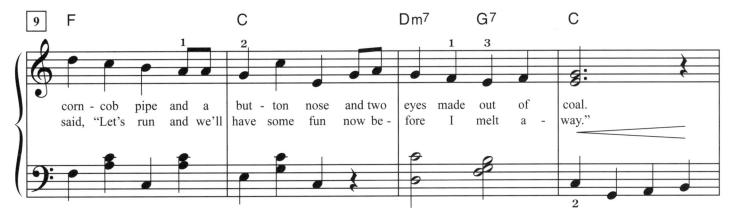

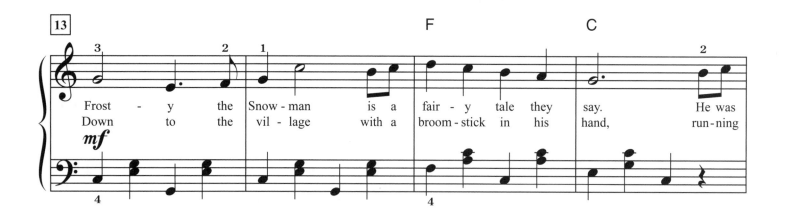

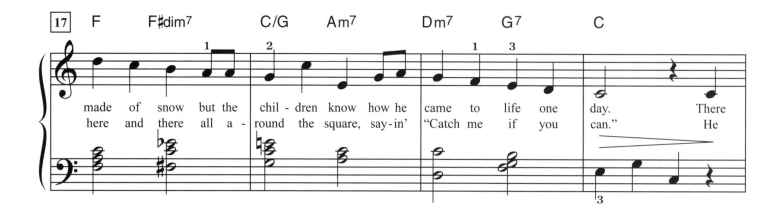

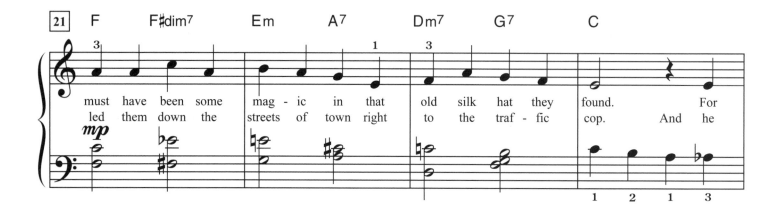

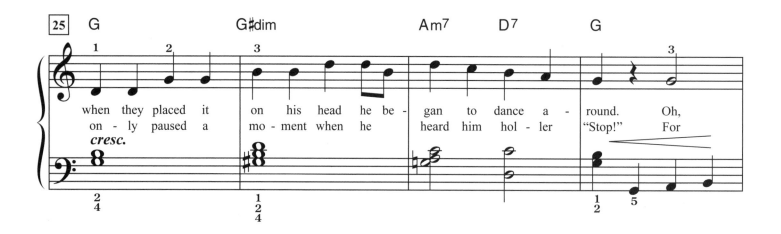

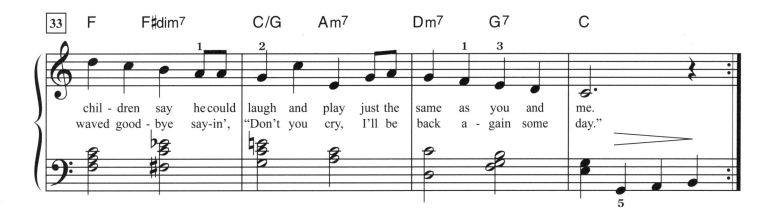

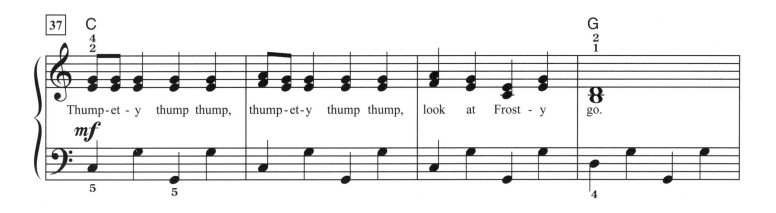

The Gift

Words and Music by
Jim Brickman and Tom Douglas
Arr. Dan Coates

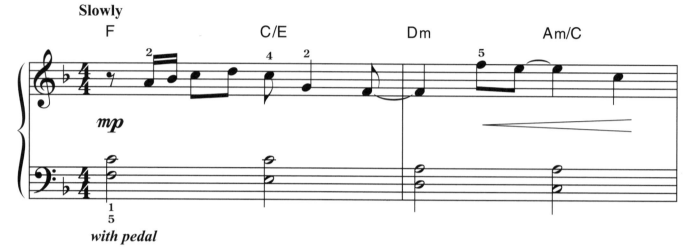

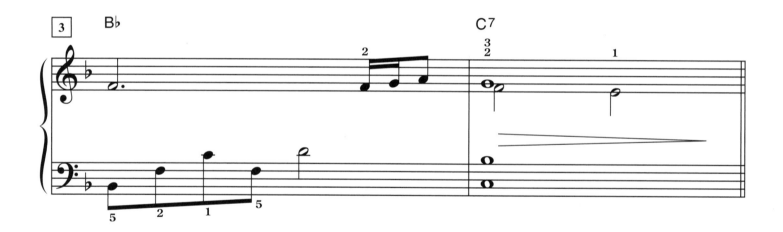

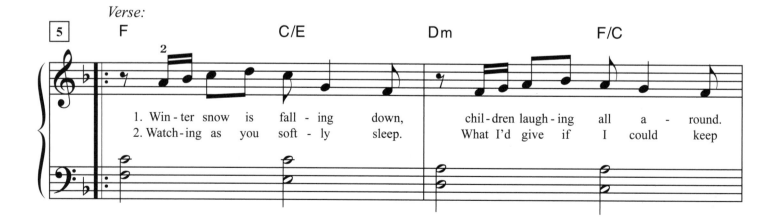

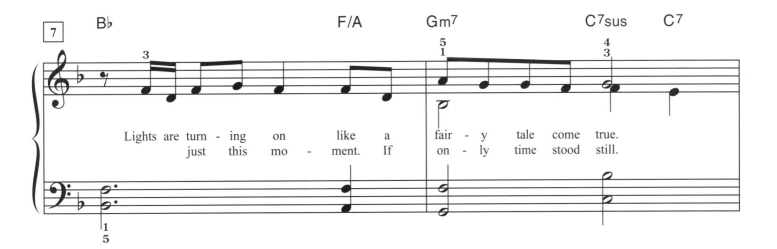

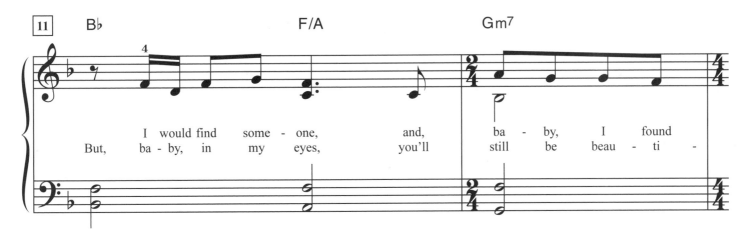

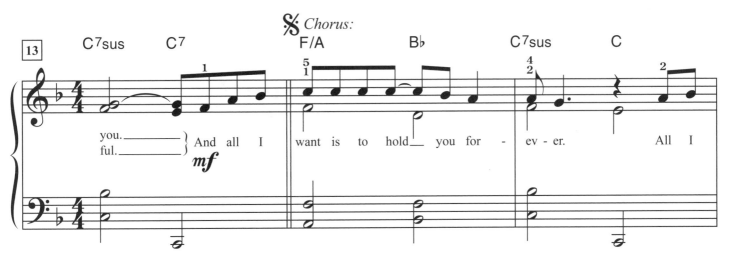

44

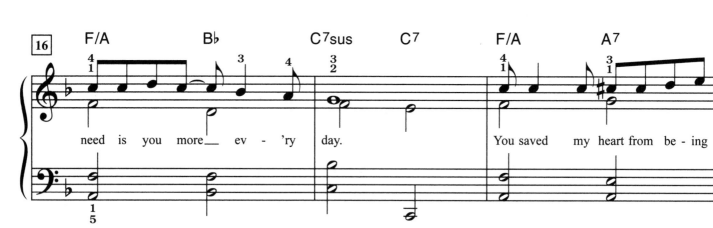

need is you more__ ev - 'ry day.   You saved   my heart from be - ing

to Coda ✛

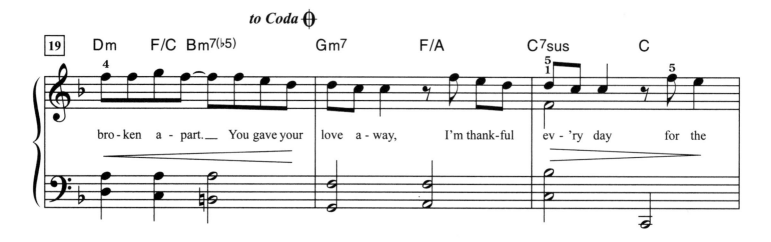

bro - ken a - part.__ You gave your   love a - way,   I'm thank - ful   ev - 'ry day   for the

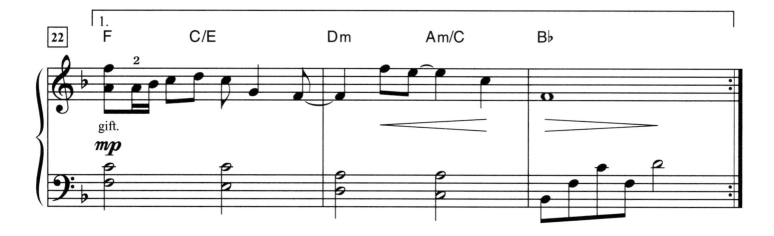

gift.

mp

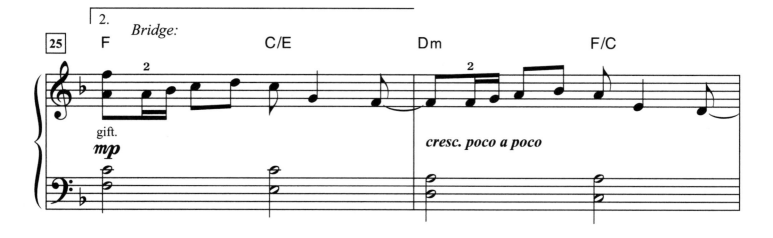

gift.

mp   *cresc. poco a poco*

D.S. al Coda

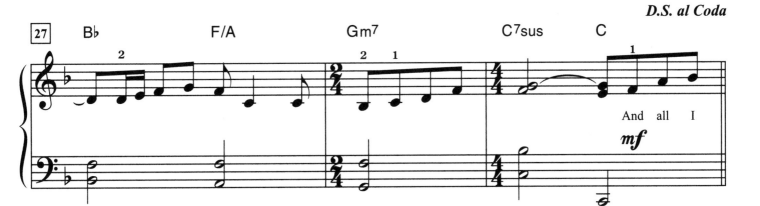

And all I

mf

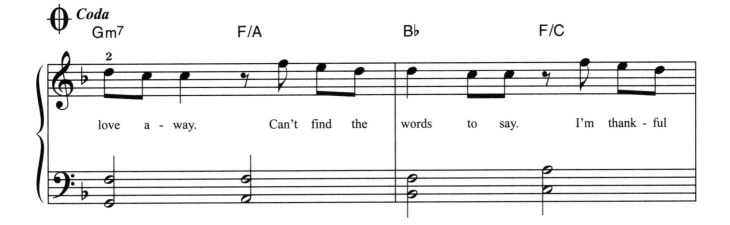

Coda

love a - way. Can't find the words to say. I'm thank - ful

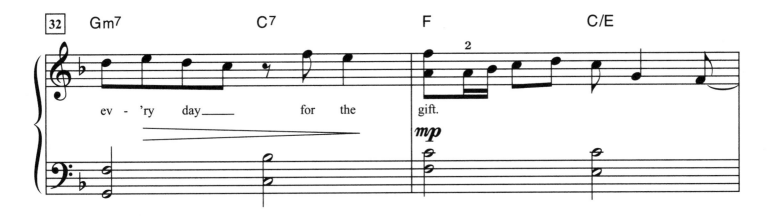

ev - 'ry day_____ for the gift.

mp

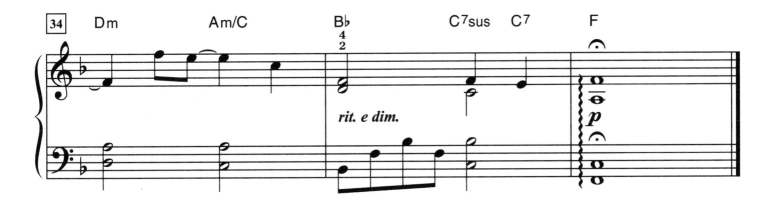

rit. e dim.

p

God Rest Ye Merry, Gentlemen

Traditional English carol
Arr. Dan Coates

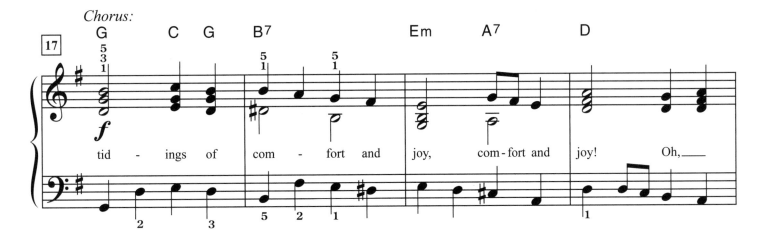

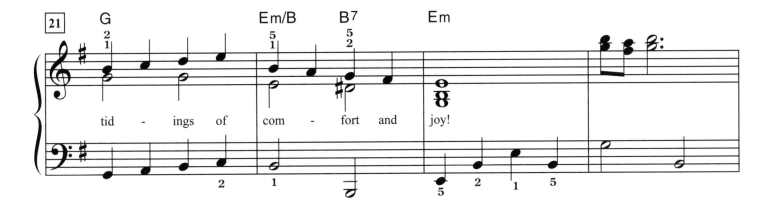

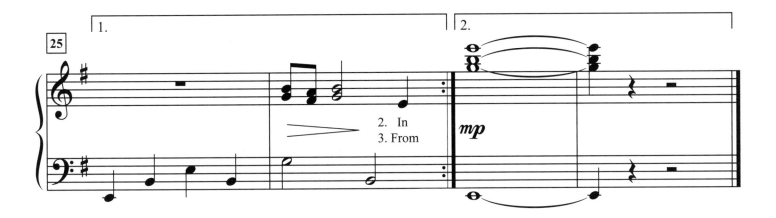

Verse 2:
In Bethlehem, in Israel, this blessed babe was born,
And laid within a manger upon this blessed morn;
The which His mother Mary did nothing take in scorn.
(To Chorus:)

Verse 3:
From God our Heavenly Father, a blessed angel came,
And unto certain shepherds brought tidings of the same;
How that in Bethlehem was born the Son of God by name.
(To Chorus:)

Good King Wenceslas

Traditional
Arr. Dan Coates

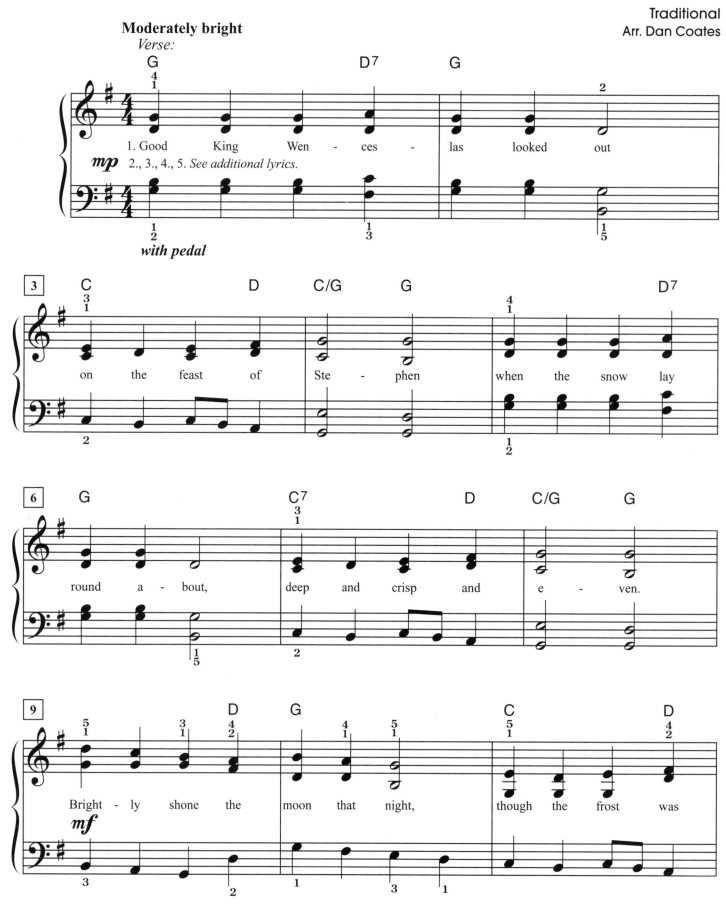

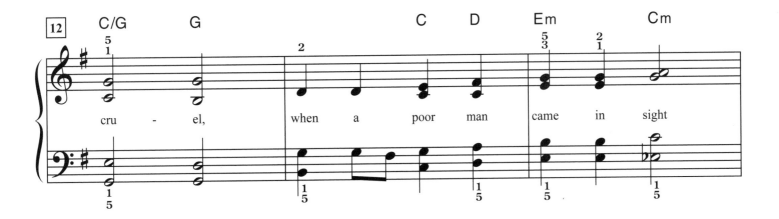

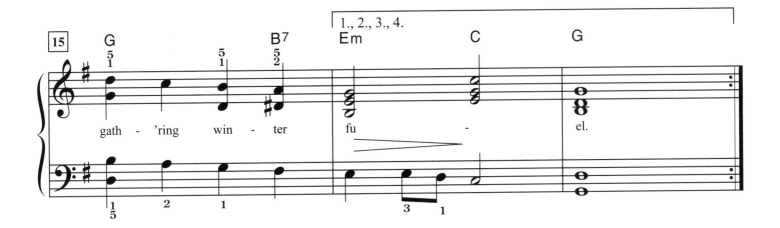

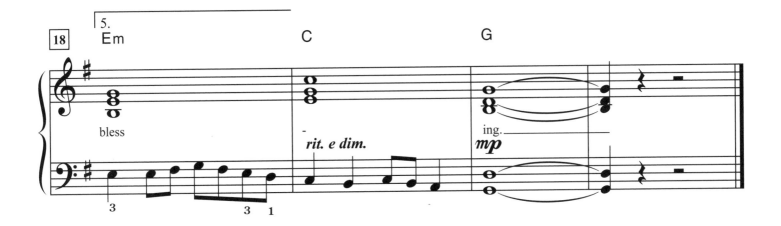

Verse 2:
"Hither, page, and stand by me, if thou know'st it, telling,
Yonder peasant, who is he? Where and what his dwelling?"
"Sire, he lives a good league hence, underneath the mountain,
Right against the forest fence, by Saint Agnes' Fountain."

Verse 3:
"Bring me flesh and bring me wine, bring me pine logs hither.
Thou and I will see him dine when we bear him thither."
Page and monarch forth they went, forth they went together,
Through the rude wind's wild lament and the bitter weather.

Verse 4:
"Sire, the night is darker now, and the wind blows stronger.
Fails my heart, I know not how, I can go no longer."
"Mark my footsteps, my good page, tread thou in them boldy.
Thou shalt find the winter's rage freeze thy blood less coldly."

Verse 5:
In his master's steps he trod, where the snow lay dinted.
Heat was in the very sod which the Saint had printed.
Therefore, Christian men, be sure, wealth or rank possessing;
Ye who now will bless the poor shall yourselves find blessing.

Grandma Got Run Over by a Reindeer

Words and Music by Randy Brooks
Arr. Dan Coates

Moderately bright
Chorus:

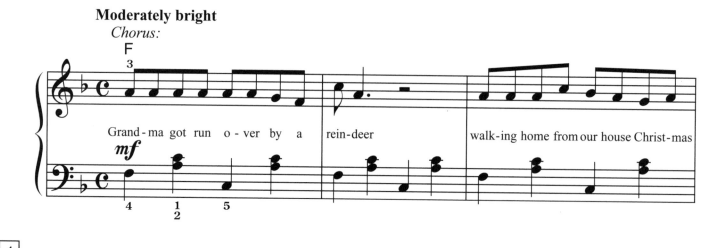

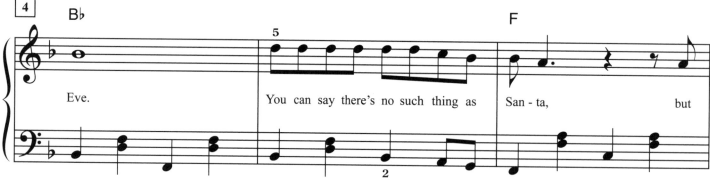

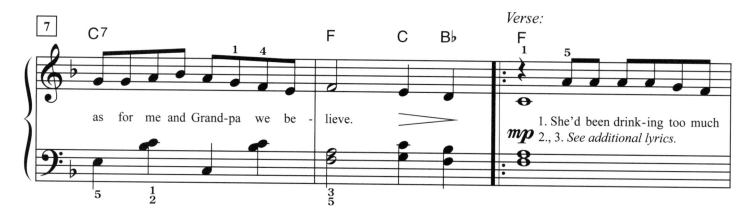

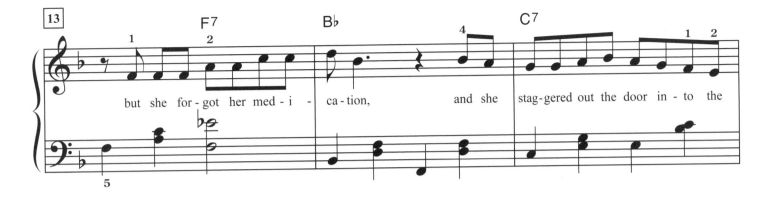

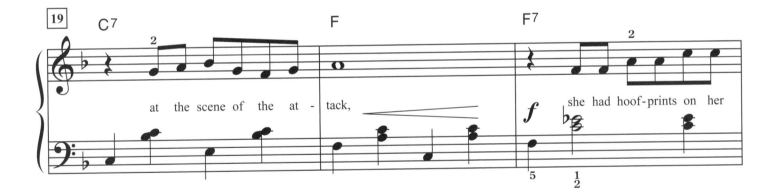

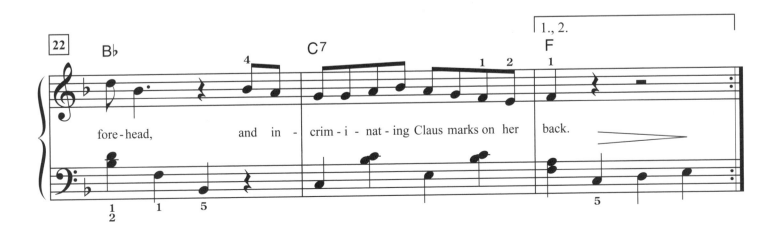

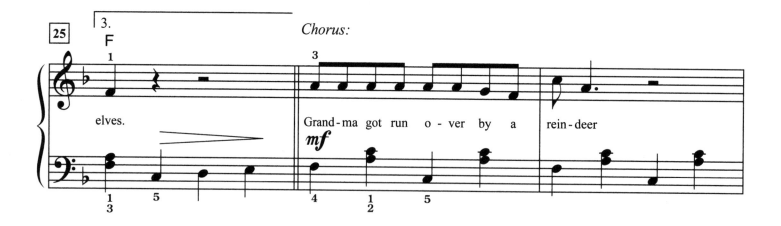

Verse 2:
Now we're all so proud of Grandpa,
He's been taking this so well.
See him in there watching football,
Drinking beer and playing cards with Cousin Mel.
It's not Christmas without Grandma.
All the family's dressed in black,
And we just can't help but wonder:
Should we open up her gifts or send them back?
(To Chorus:)

Verse 3:
Now the goose is on the table,
And the pudding made of fig,
And the blue and silver candles,
That would just have matched the hair in Grandma's wig.
I've warned all my friends and neighbors,
Better watch out for yourselves.
They should never give a licence
To a man who drives a sleigh and plays with elves.
(To Chorus:)

Hark! the Herald Angels Sing

Felix Mendelssohn
Arr. Dan Coates

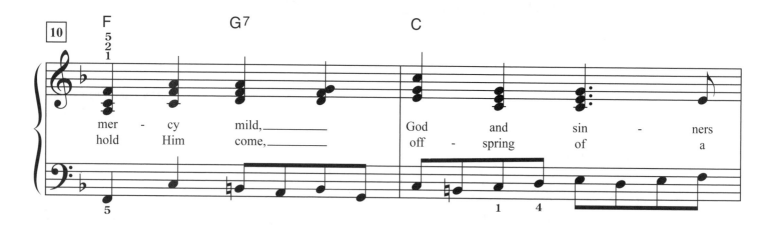

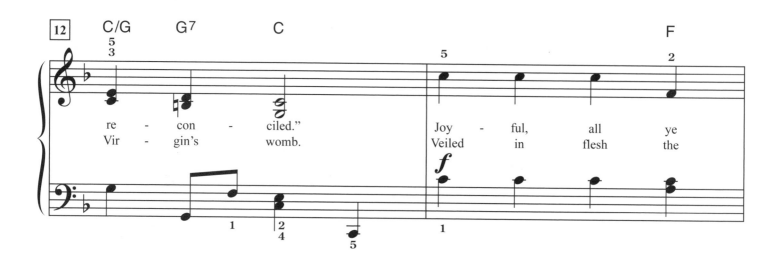

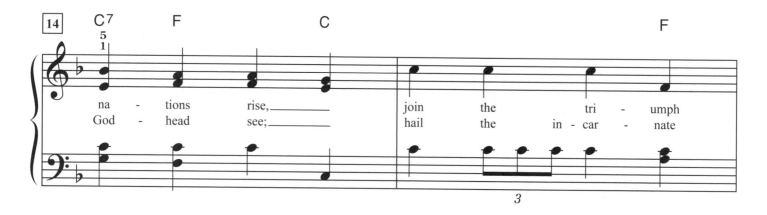

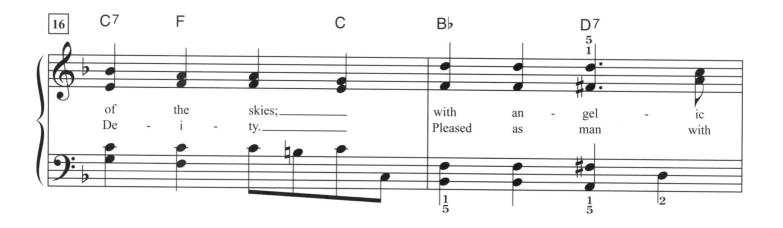

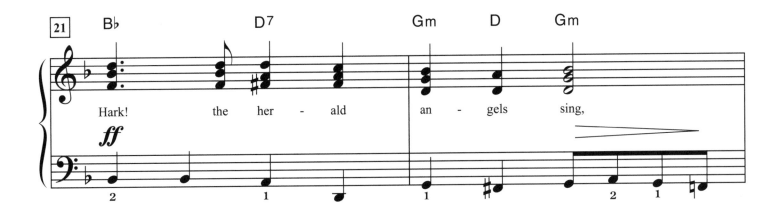

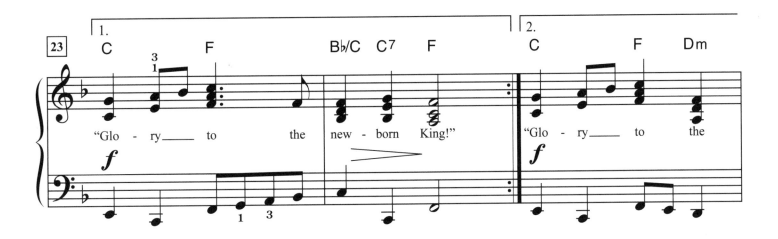

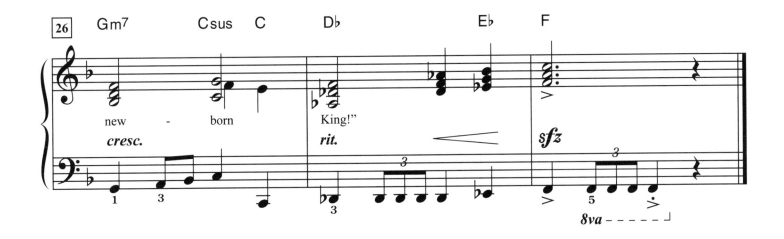

Have Yourself a Merry Little Christmas

Words and Music by
Hugh Martin and Ralph Blane
Arr. Dan Coates

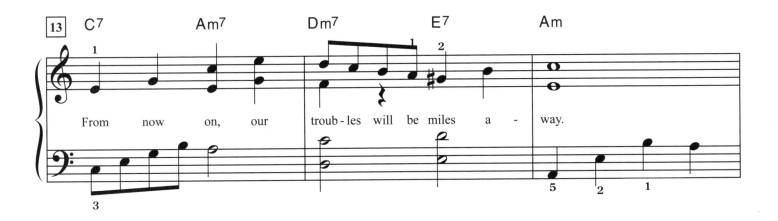

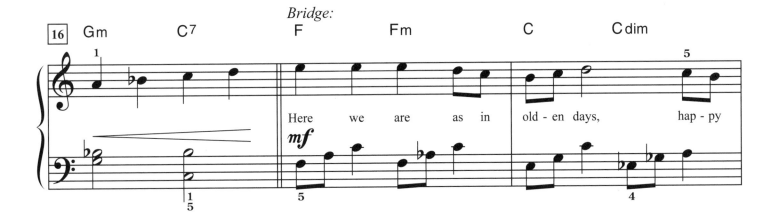

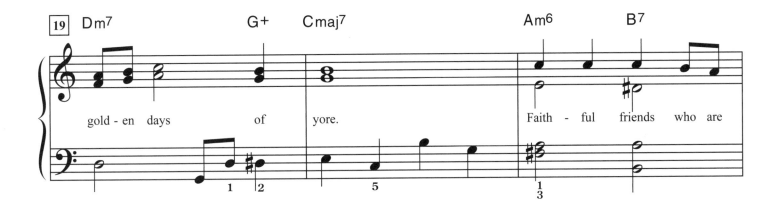

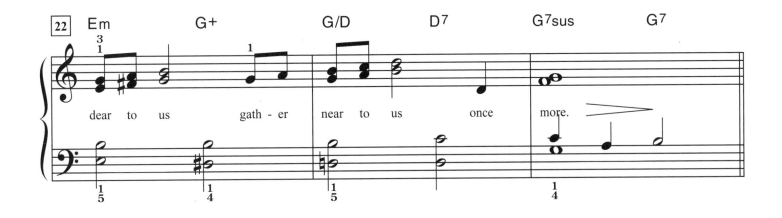

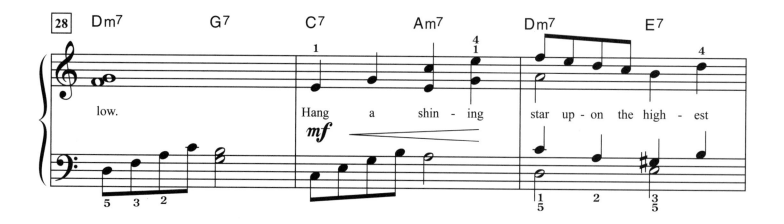

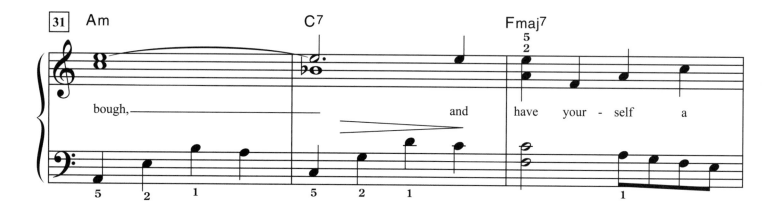

Happy Xmas (War Is Over)

Words and Music by
John Lennon and Yoko Ono
Arr. Dan Coates

the near and the dear ones,_____ the old and the
the near and the dear ones,_____ the old and the

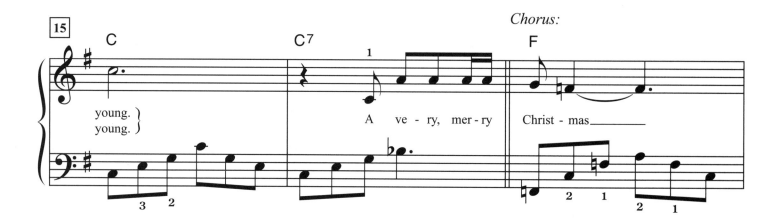

Chorus:

young.
young.

A ve-ry, mer-ry Christ-mas_____

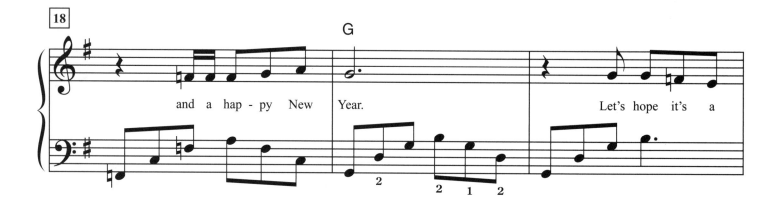

and a hap-py New Year.

Let's hope it's a

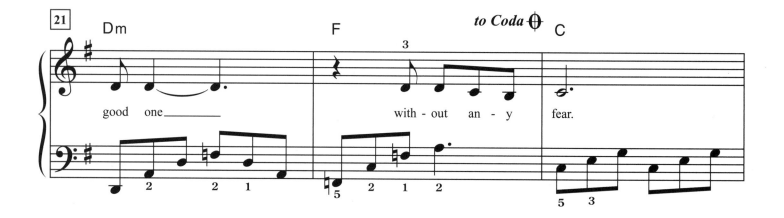

to Coda

good one_____ with-out an-y fear.

61

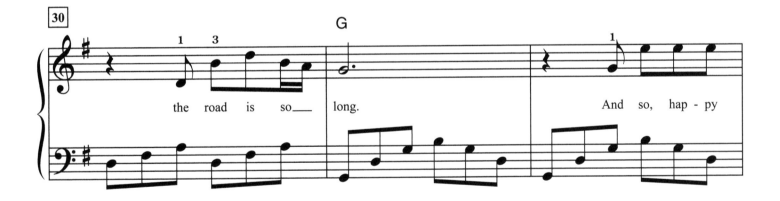

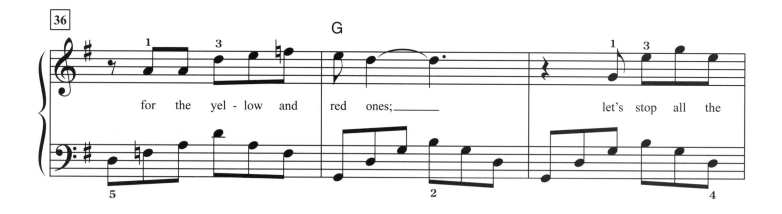

for the yel - low and red ones;_____ let's stop all the

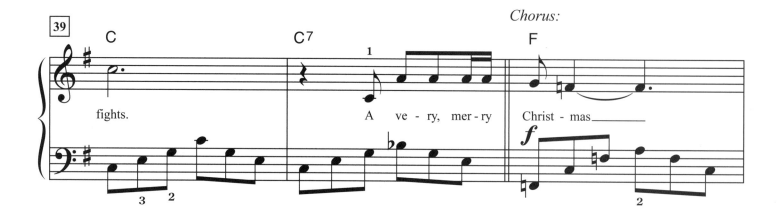

Chorus:

fights. A ve - ry, mer - ry Christ - mas_____

and a hap - py New Year. Let's hope it's a

good one_____ with - out an - y fear.

D.S. al Coda

Coda

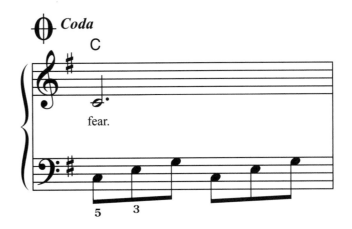

3. And so this is

fear.

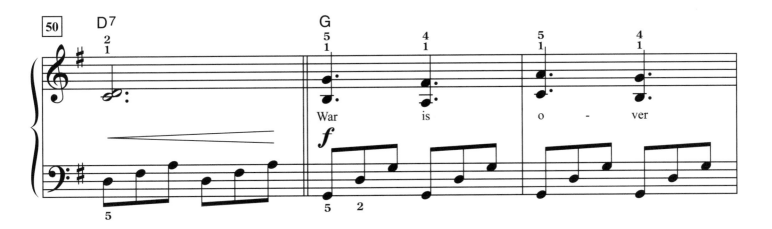

War is o - ver

if you want it; war is

o - ver now.

A Holly Jolly Christmas

Words and Music by Johnny Marks
Arr. Dan Coates

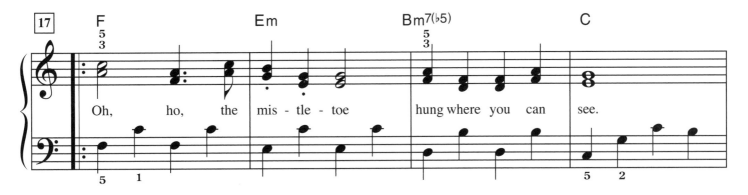

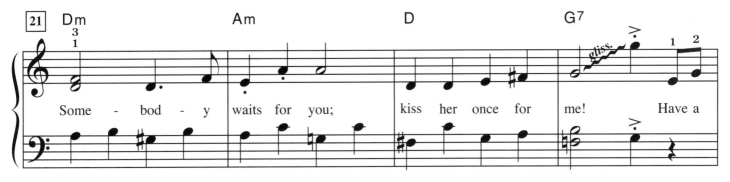

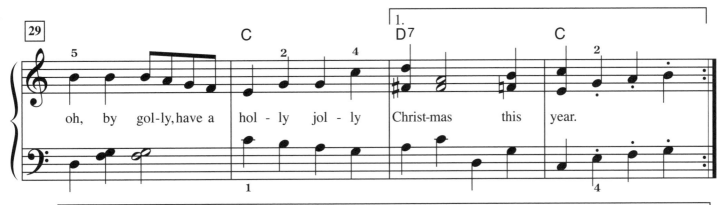

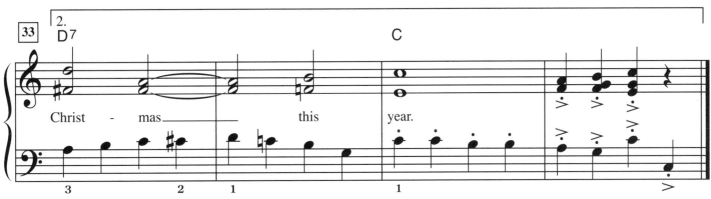

I Saw Three Ships

Traditional English Carol
Arr. Dan Coates

Moderately bright

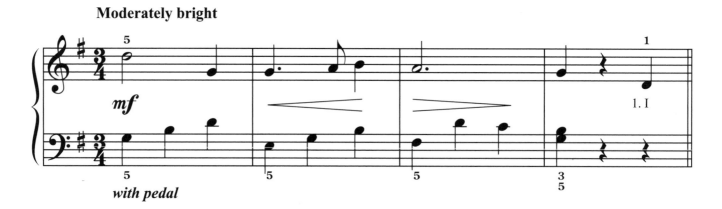

with pedal

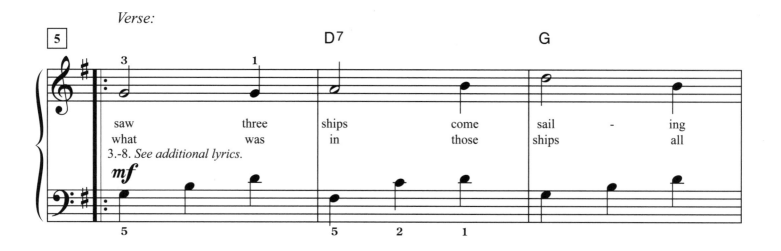

Verse:

saw   three   ships   come   sail - ing

what   was   in   those   ships   all

3.-8. *See additional lyrics.*

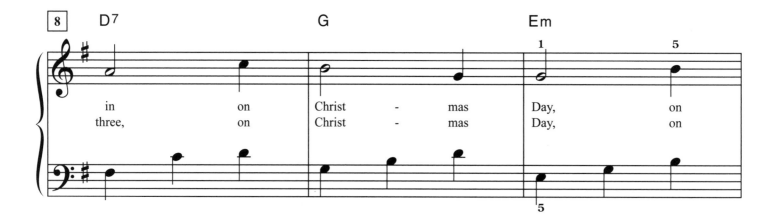

in   on   Christ - mas   Day,   on

three,   on   Christ - mas   Day,   on

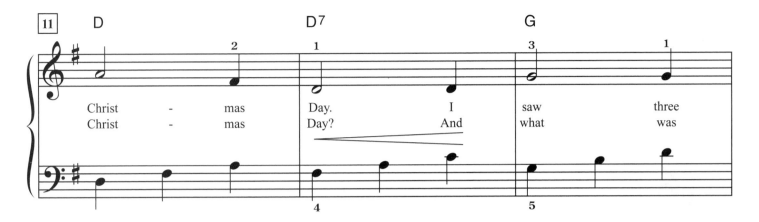

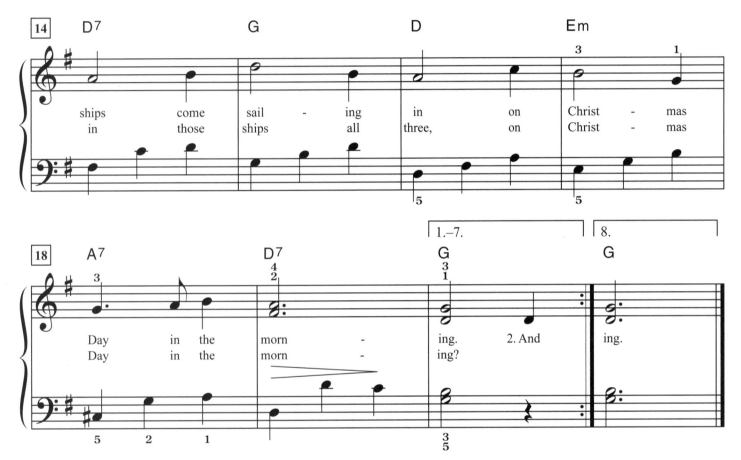

Verse 3:
The Virgin Mary and Christ were there,
On Christmas Day, on Christmas Day.
The Virgin Mary and Christ were there,
On Christmas Day in the morning.

Verse 4:
Pray, wither sailed those ships all three,
On Christmas Day, on Christmas Day?
Pray, wither sailed those ships all three,
On Christmas Day in the morning?

Verse 5:
O they sailed into Bethlehem,
On Christmas Day, on Christmas Day.
O they sailed into Bethlehem,
On Christmas Day in the morning.

Verse 6:
And all the bells on earth shall ring,
On Christmas day, on Christmas Day.
And all the bells on earth shall ring,
On Christmas Day in the morning.

Verse 7:
And all the angels in heaven shall sing,
On Christmas Day, on Christmas Day.
And all the angels in heaven shall sing,
On Christmas Day in the morning.

Verse 8:
Then let us all rejoice again,
On Christmas Day, on Christmas Day.
Then let us all rejoice again,
On Christmas Day in the morning.

It Came Upon the Midnight Clear

Richard S. Willis
Arr. Dan Coates

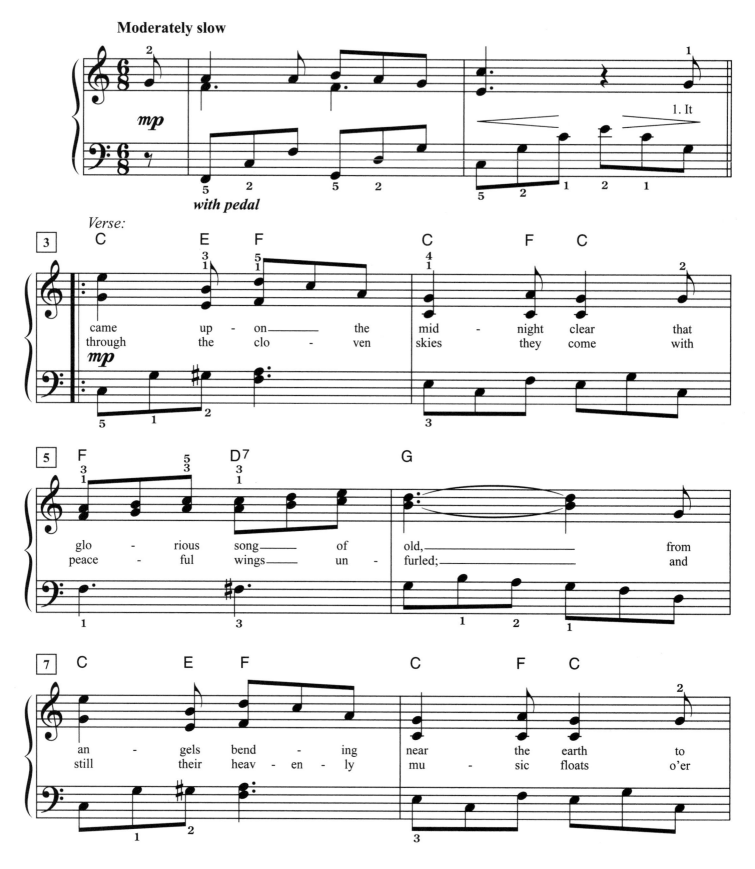

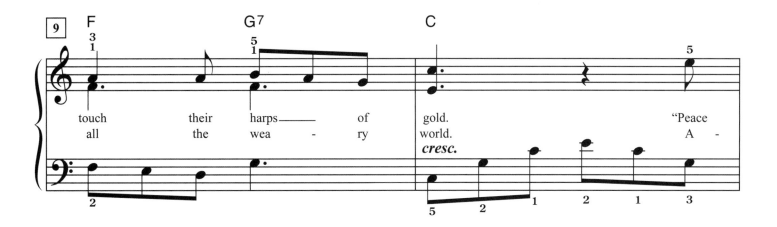

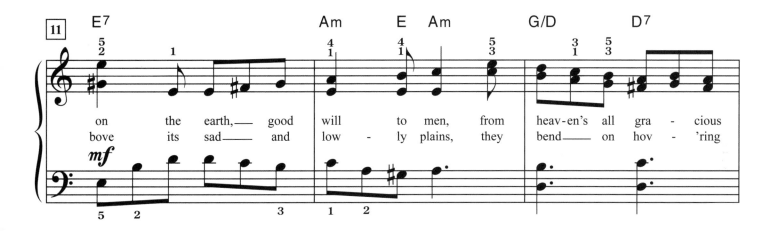

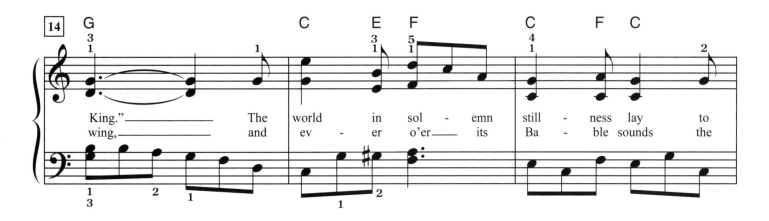

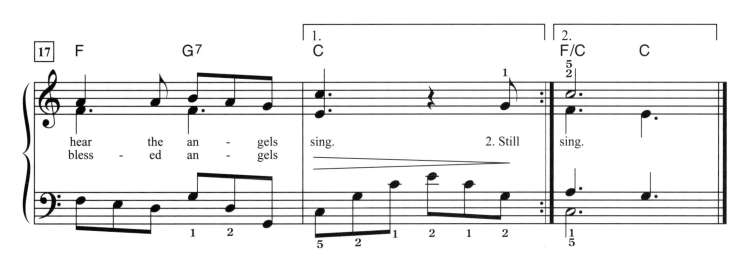

It's the Most Wonderful Time of the Year

Words and Music by
Eddie Pola and George Wyle
Arr. Dan Coates

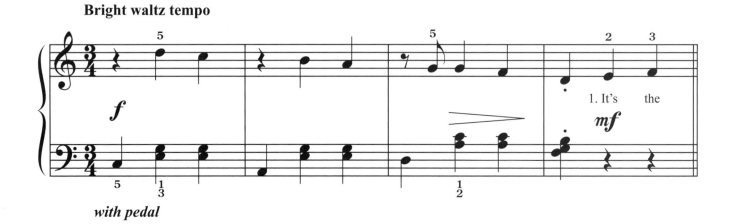

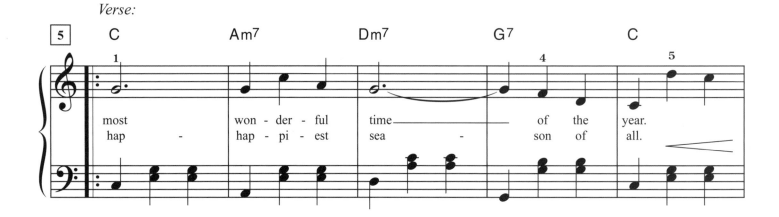

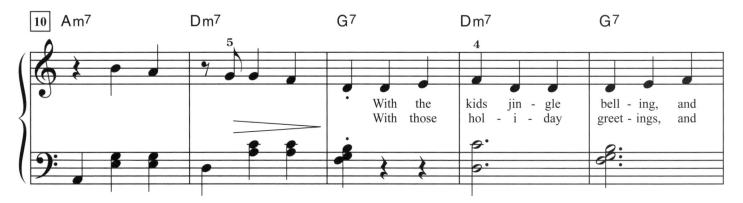

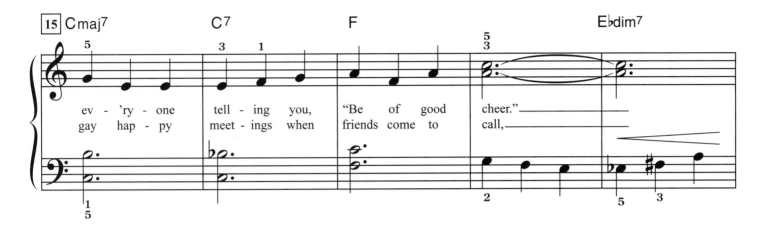

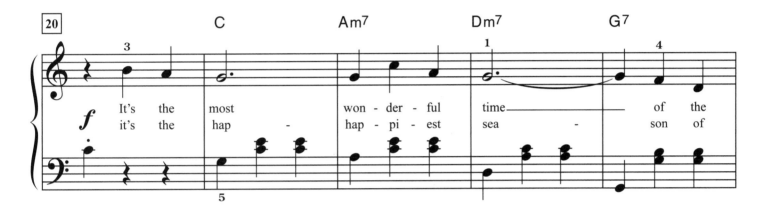

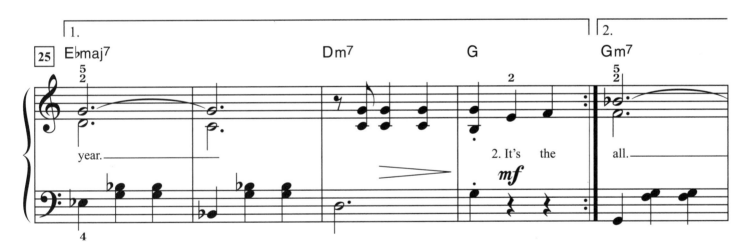

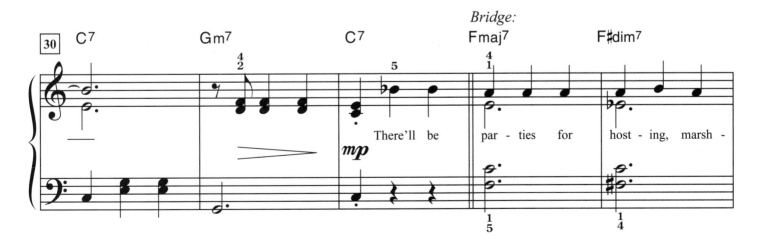

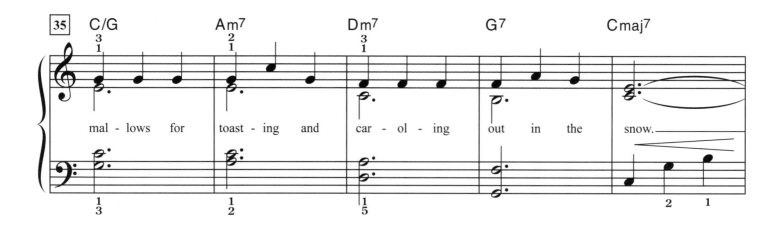

mal - lows for toast - ing and car - ol - ing out in the snow.

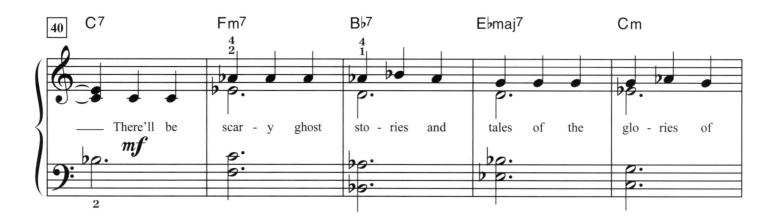

There'll be scar - y ghost sto - ries and tales of the glo - ries of

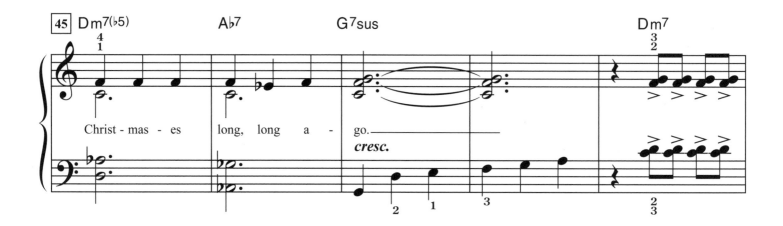

Christ - mas - es long, long a - go.

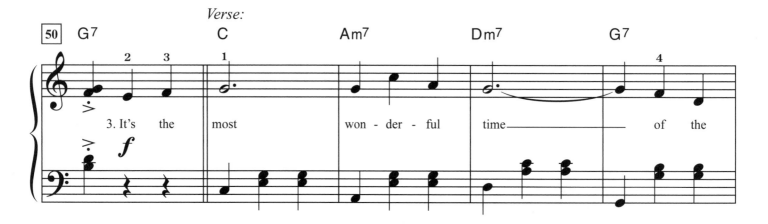

3. It's the most won - der - ful time of the

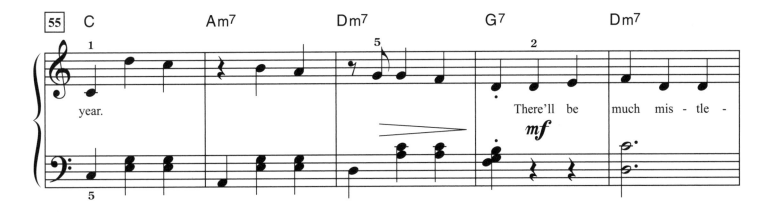

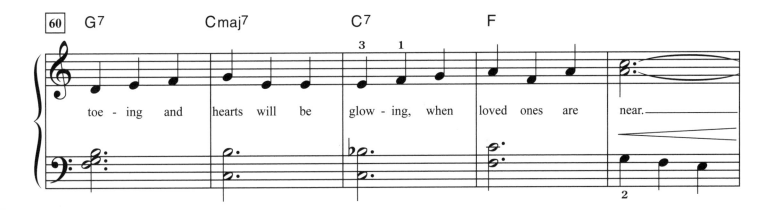

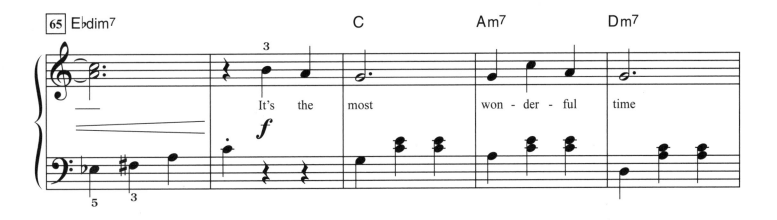

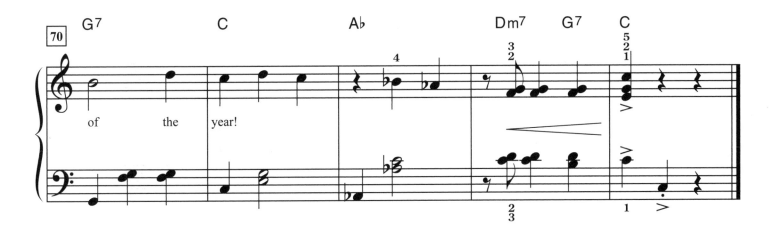

Jesu, Joy of Man's Desiring

Composed by J. S. Bach
Arr. Dan Coates

Moderately slow

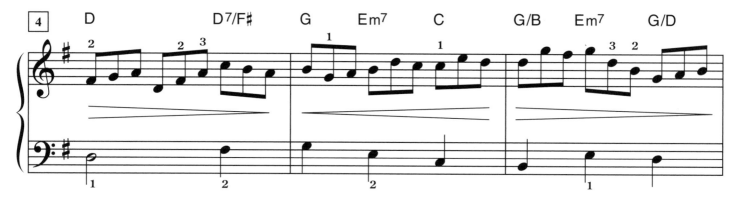

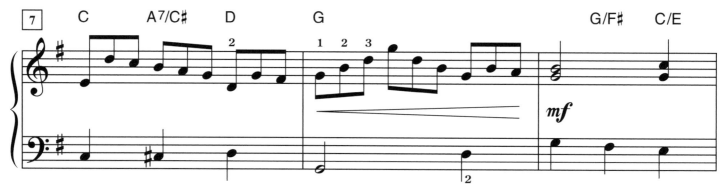

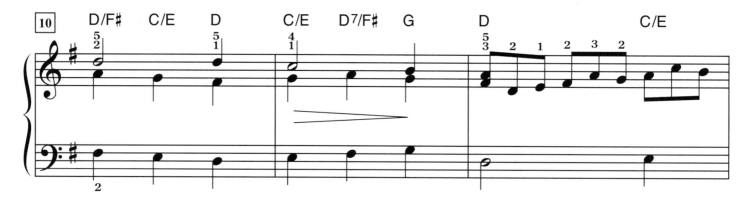

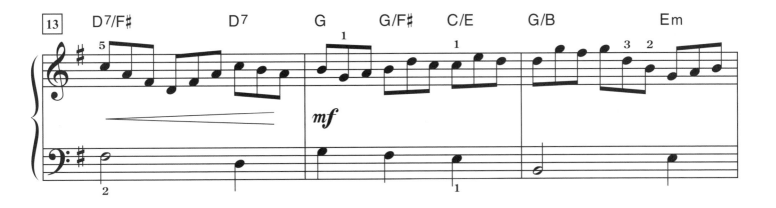

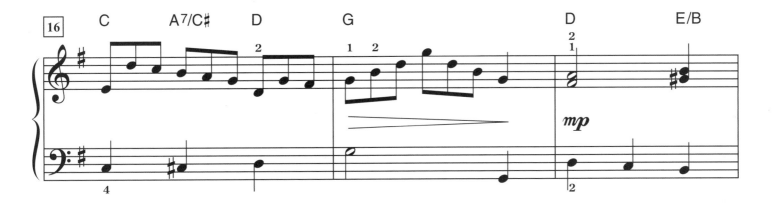

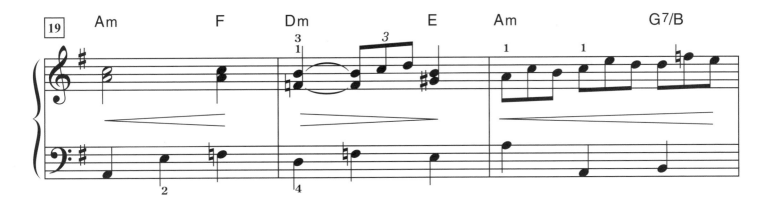

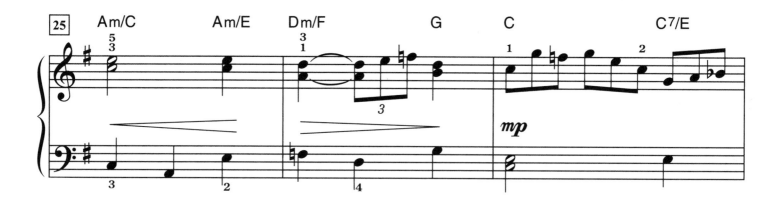

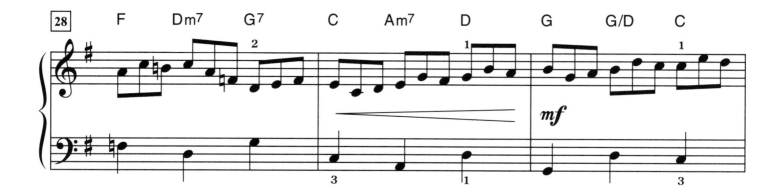

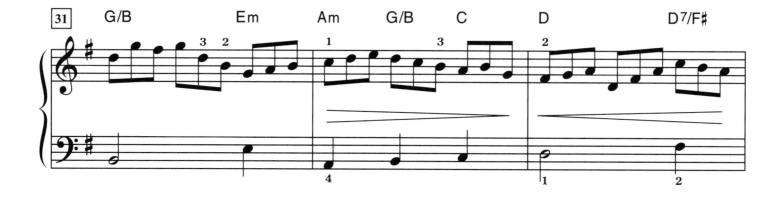

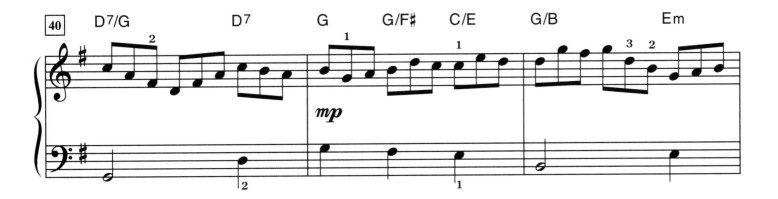

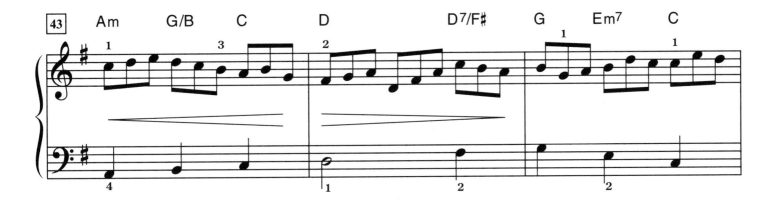

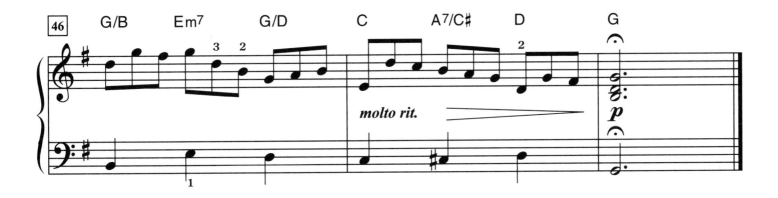

Jingle Bells

Words and Music by James Pierpont
Arr. Dan Coates

Dash - ing through the snow in a one - horse o - pen sleigh;

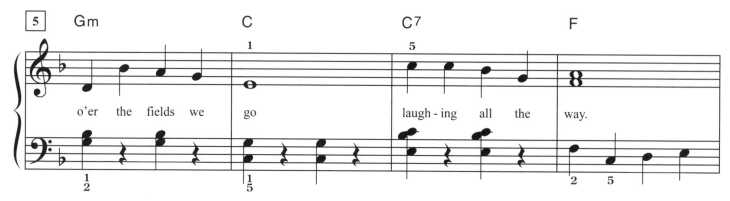

o'er the fields we go laugh - ing all the way.

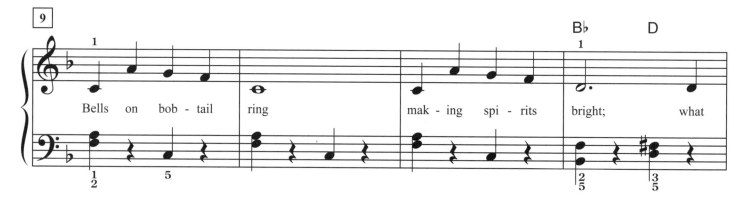

Bells on bob - tail ring mak - ing spi - rits bright; what

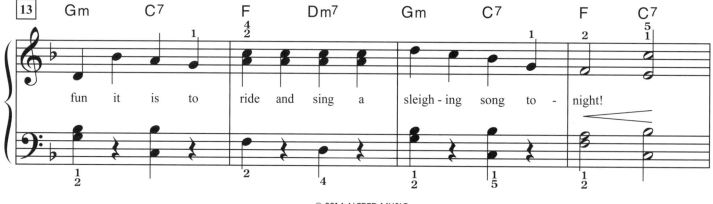

fun it is to ride and sing a sleigh - ing song to - night!

Chorus:

Jin - gle bells, jin - gle bells, jin - gle all the way.

Oh, what fun it is to ride in a one - horse o - pen sleigh!

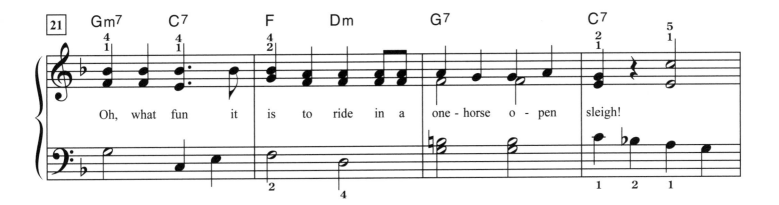

Jin - gle bells, jin - gle bells, jin - gle all the way.

Oh, what fun it is to ride in a one - horse o - pen sleigh!

(There's No Place Like)
Home for the Holidays

Words by Al Stillman
Music by Robert Allen
Arr. Dan Coates

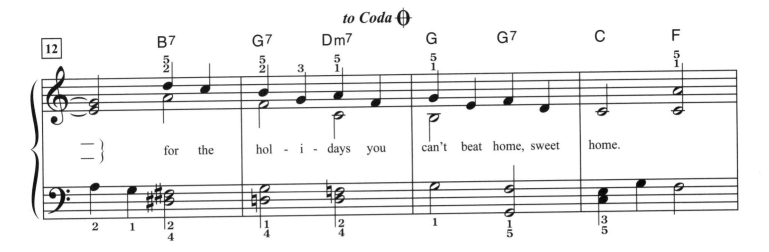

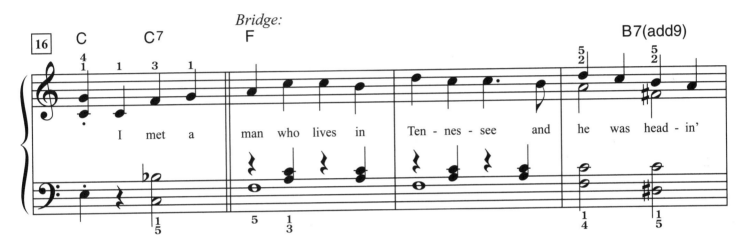

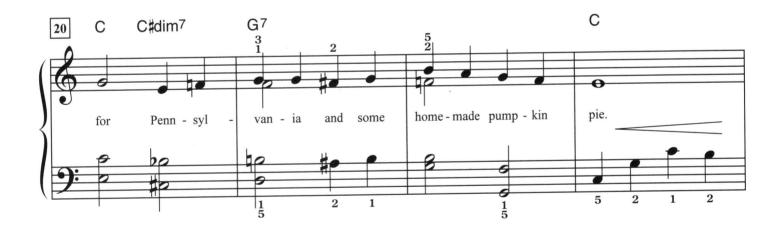

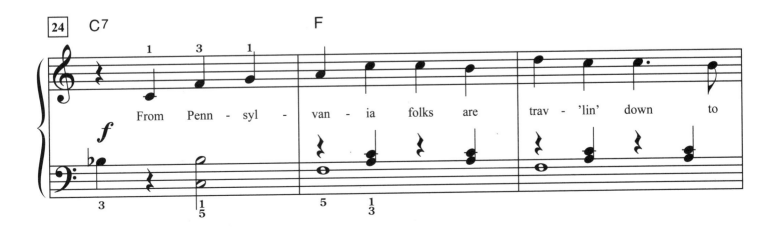

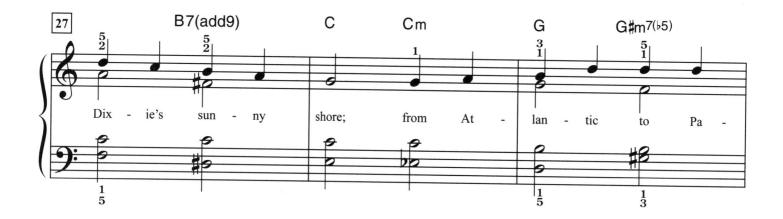

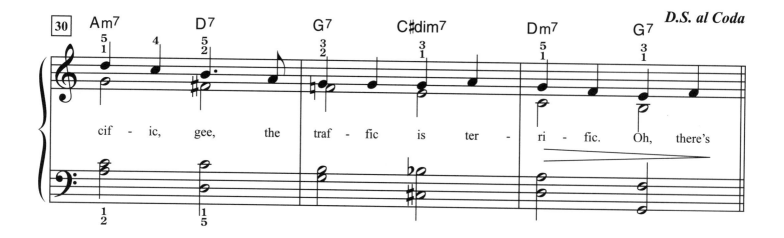

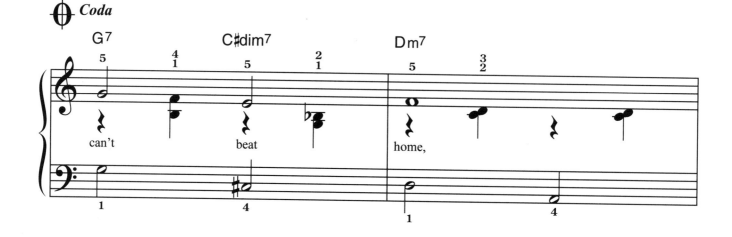

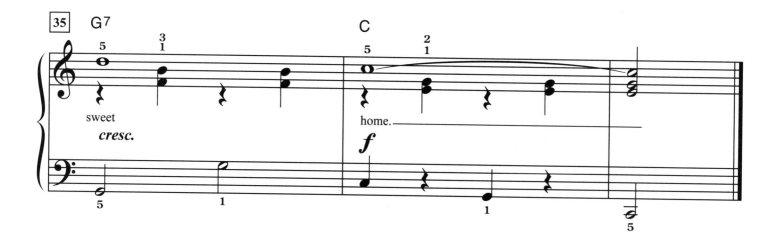

Jingle Bell Rock

Words and Music by
Joe Beal and Jim Boothe
Arr. Dan Coates

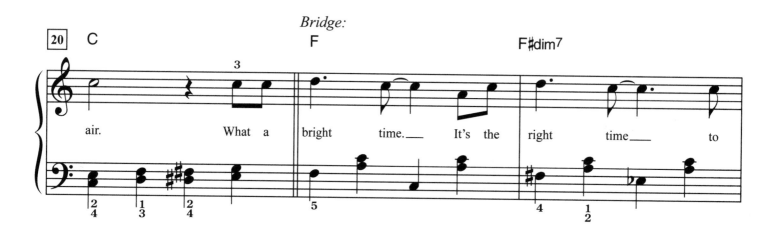

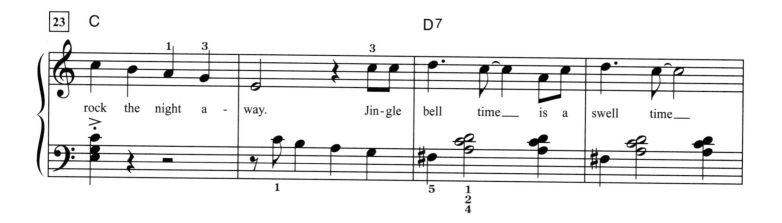

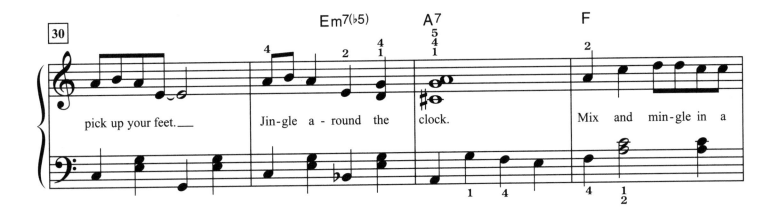

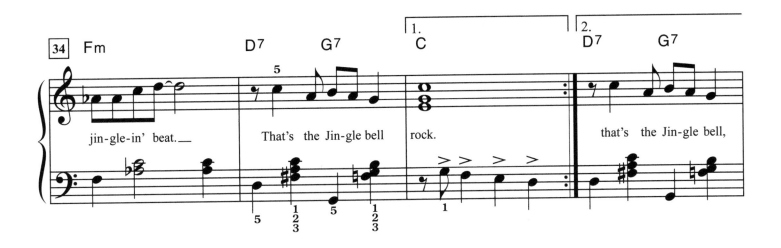

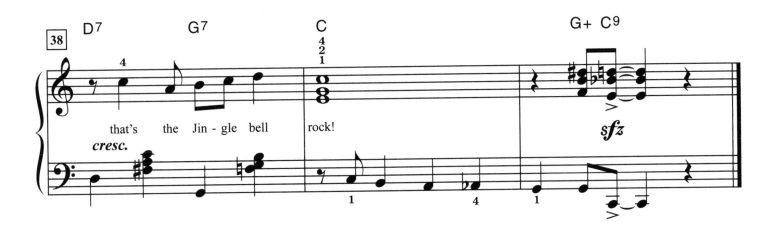

Jolly Old Saint Nicholas

Traditional
Arr. Dan Coates

Joy to the World

Music by Lowell Mason
Words by Isaac Watts
Arr. Dan Coates

Majestically

Joy to the world! The Lord has come. Let earth re-
Joy to the world! The Sav - ior reigns. Let men their

ceive her King. Let ev - 'ry heart pre - pare Him
songs em - ploy. While fields and floods, rock, hills and

room. And heav'n and na - ture sing, and heav'n and na - ture sing, and
plains re - peat the sound - ing joy, re - peat the sound - ing joy, re-

heav - en and heav - en and na - ture sing.
peat, and re - peat the sound - ing joy.

Let It Snow! Let It Snow! Let It Snow!

Words by Sammy Cahn
Music by Jule Styne
Arr. Dan Coates

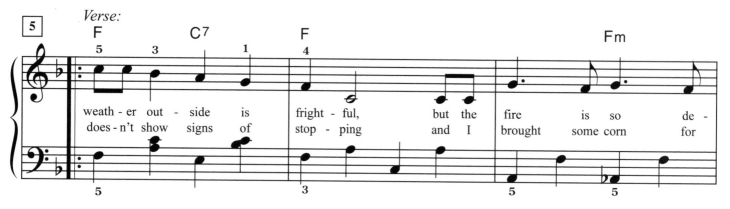

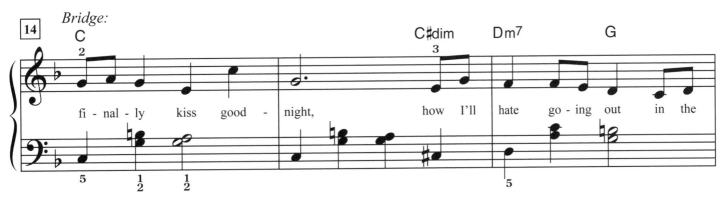

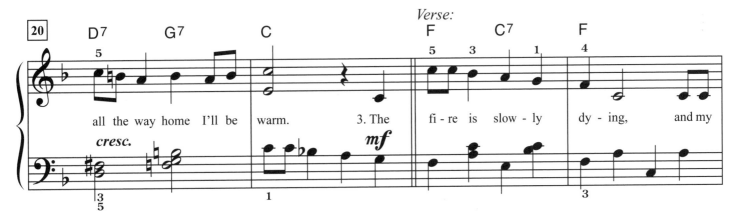

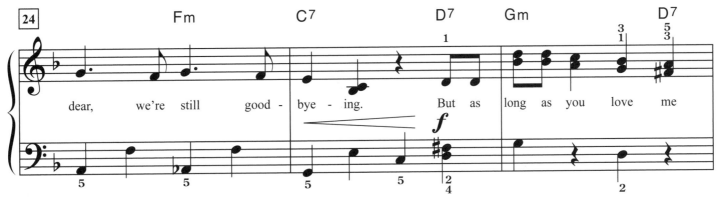

I'll Be Home for Christmas

Words by Kim Gannon
Music by Walter Kent
Arr. Dan Coates

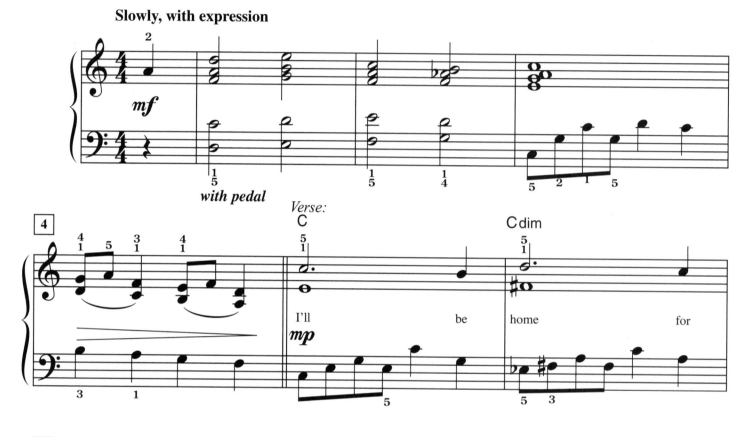

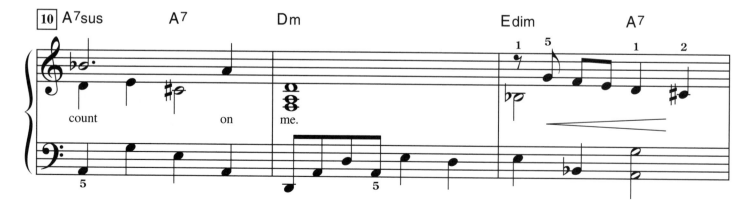

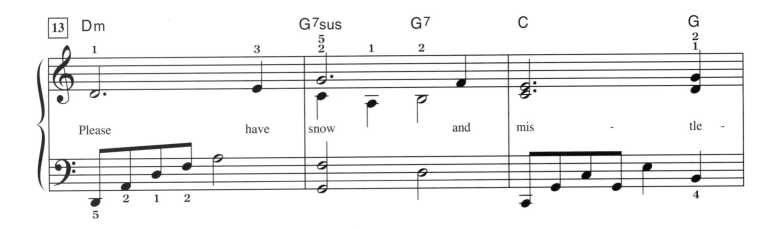

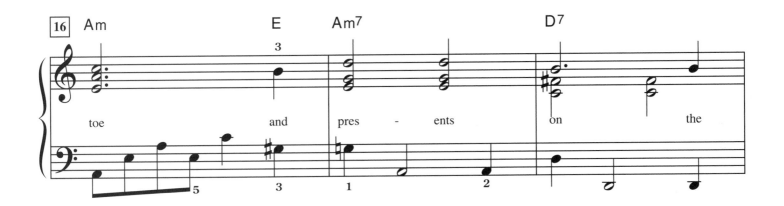

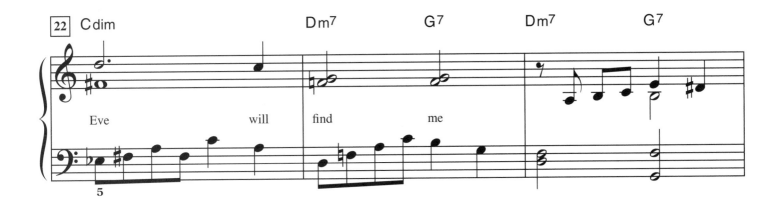

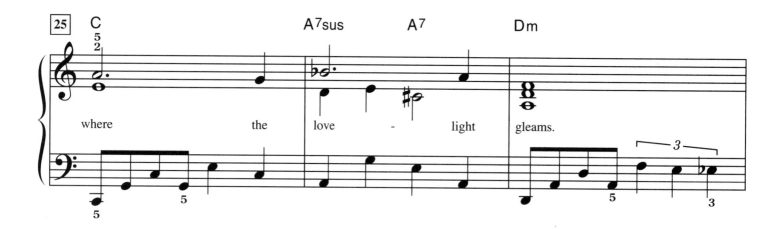

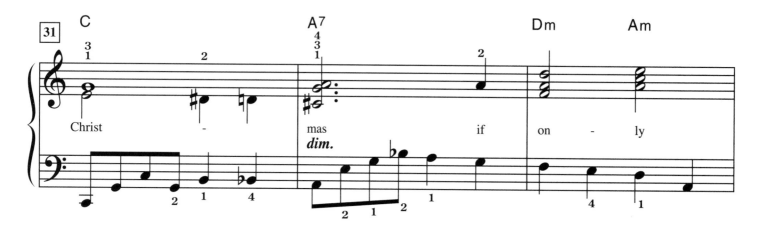

The Little Drummer Boy

Words and Music by Harry Simeone,
Henry Onorati and Katherine Davis
Arr. Dan Coates

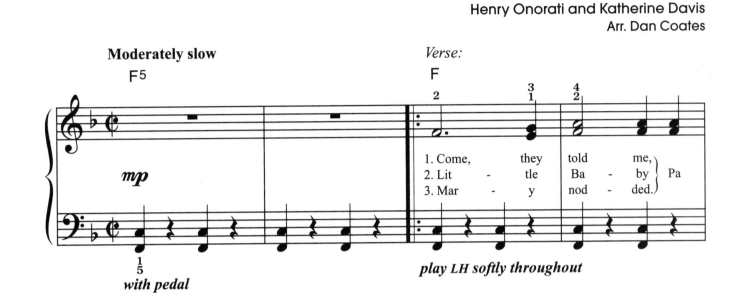

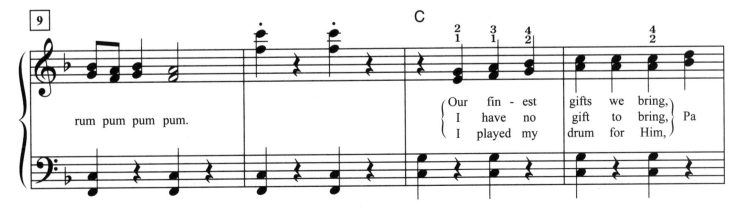

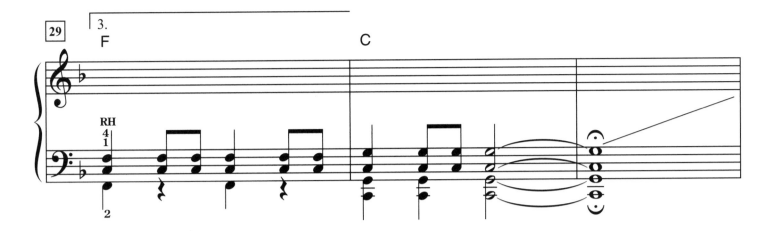

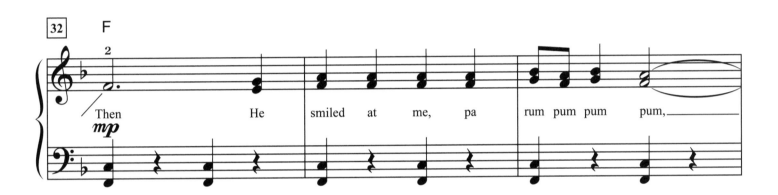

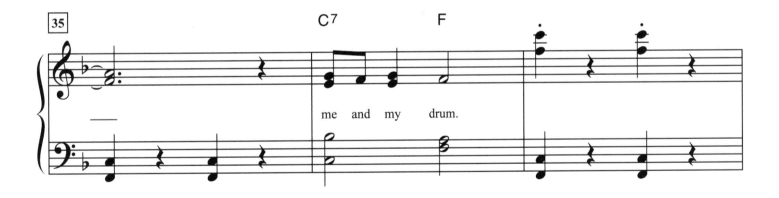

Mele Kalikimaka

Words and Music by R. Alex Anderson
Arr. Dan Coates

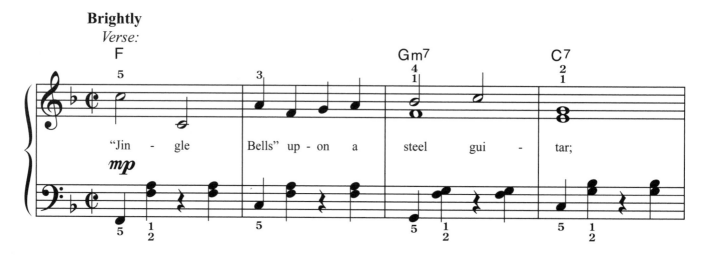

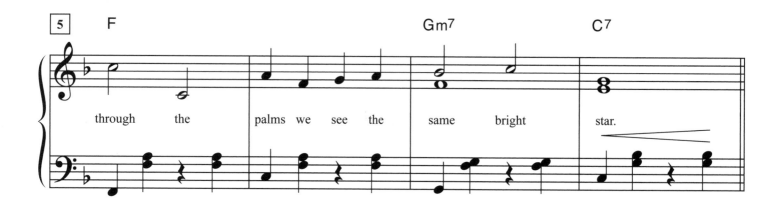

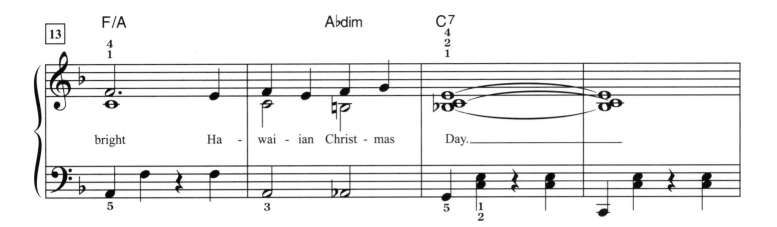

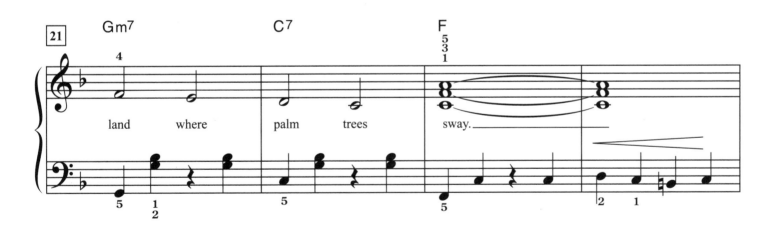

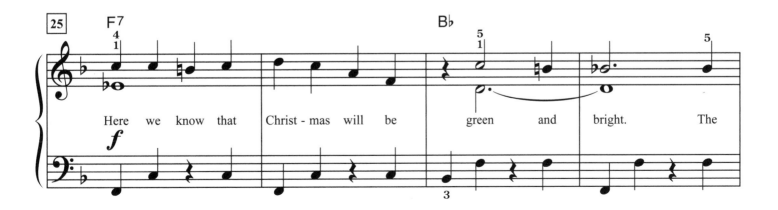

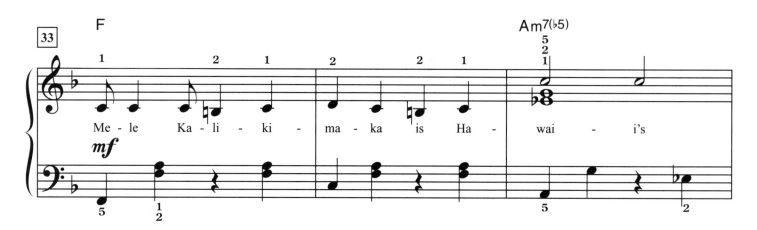

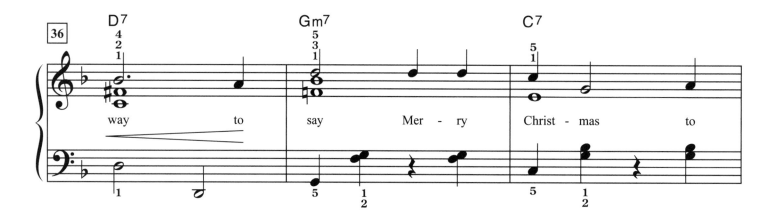

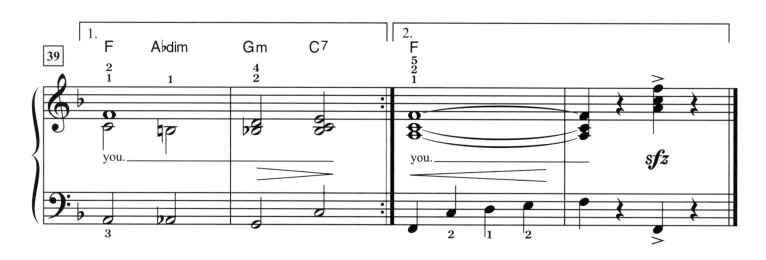

Nuttin' for Christmas

Words and Music by
Sid Tepper and Roy C. Bennett
Arr. Dan Coates

Chorus:

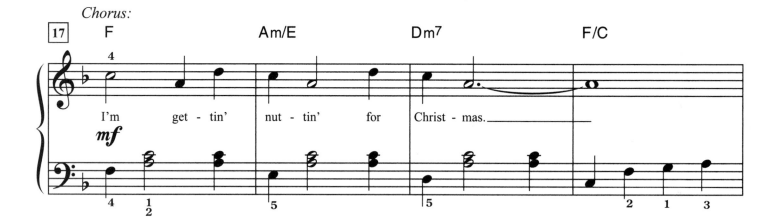

I'm get - tin' nut - tin' for Christ - mas.

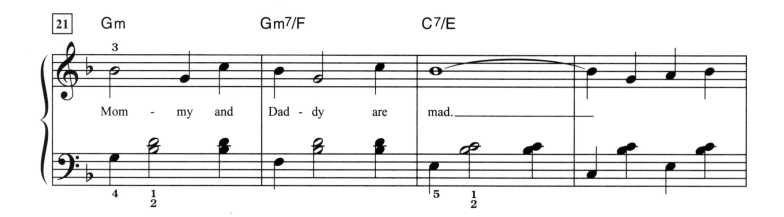

Mom - my and Dad - dy are mad.

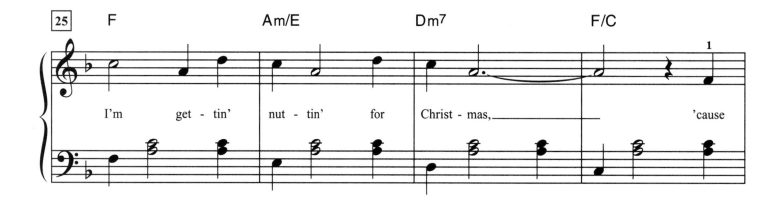

I'm get - tin' nut - tin' for Christ - mas, 'cause

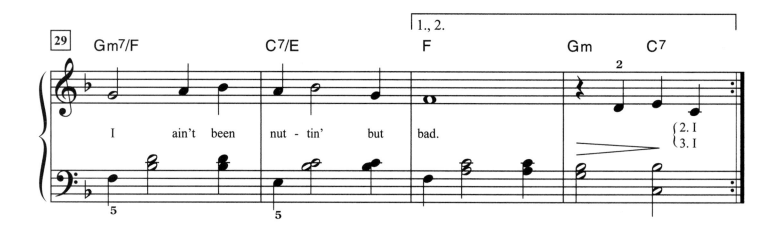

I ain't been nut - tin' but bad.

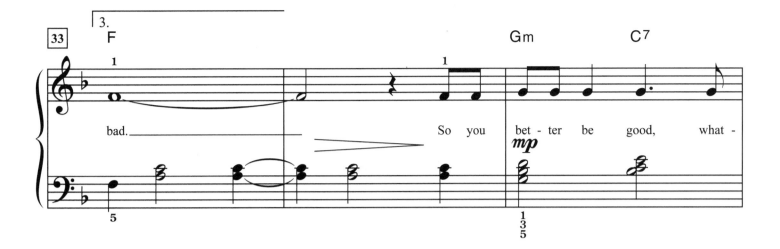

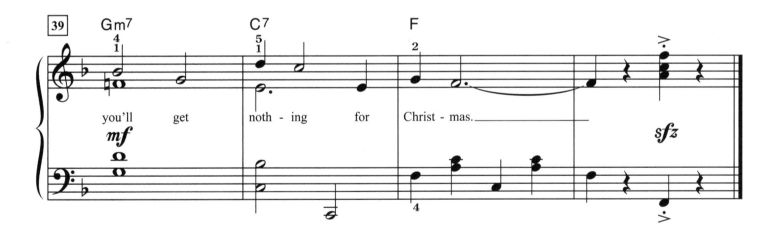

Verse 2:
I put a tack on teacher's chair;
Somebody snitched on me.
I tied a knot in Susie's hair;
Somebody snitched on me.
I did a dance on Mommy's plants,
Climbed a tree and tore my pants,
Filled the sugar bowl with ants;
Somebody snitched on me.
(To Chorus:)

Verse 3:
I won't be seeing Santa Claus;
Somebody snitched on me.
He won't come visit me because
Somebody snitched on me.
Next year I'll be going straight,
Next year I'll be good, just wait.
I'd start now but it's too late;
Somebody snitched on me.
(To Chorus:)

O Christmas Tree
(O Tannenbaum)

Traditional German carol
Arr. Dan Coates

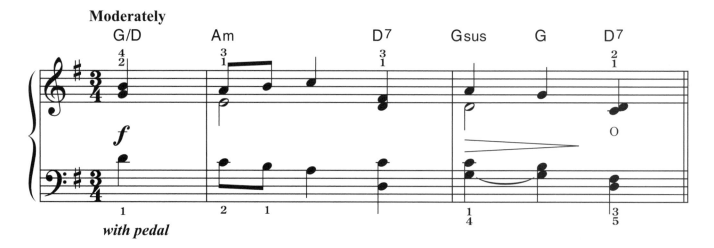

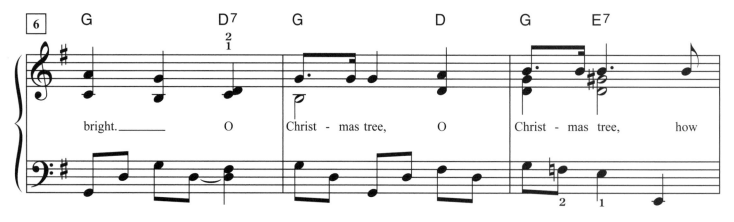

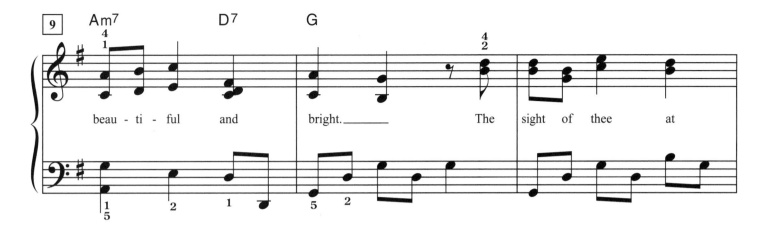

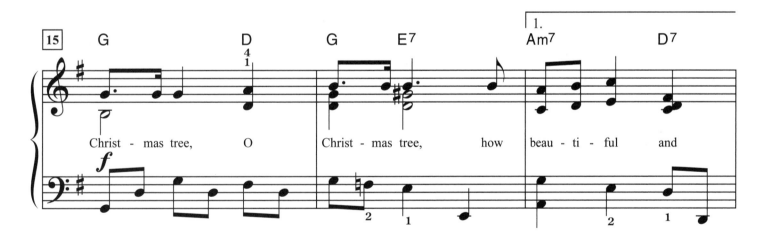

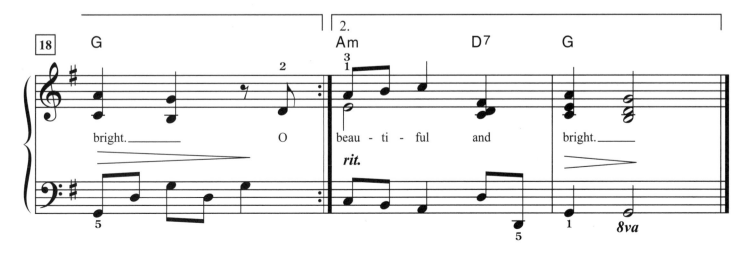

O Come, All Ye Faithful

Words by Frederick Oakeley
Music by John Francis Wade
Arr. Dan Coates

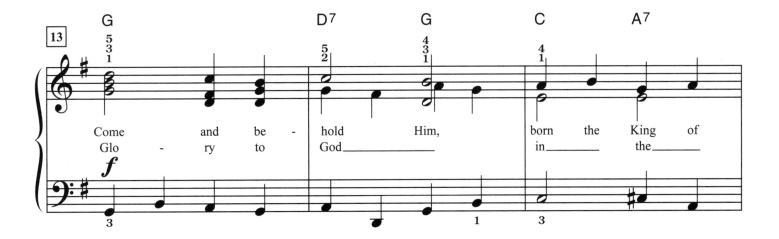

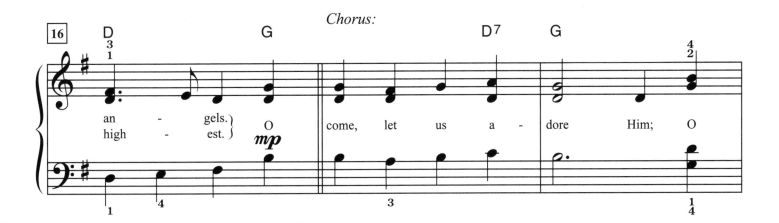

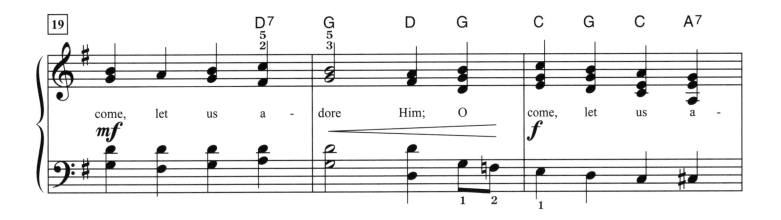

O Come, O Come Emmanuel

Plainsong
Arr. Dan Coates

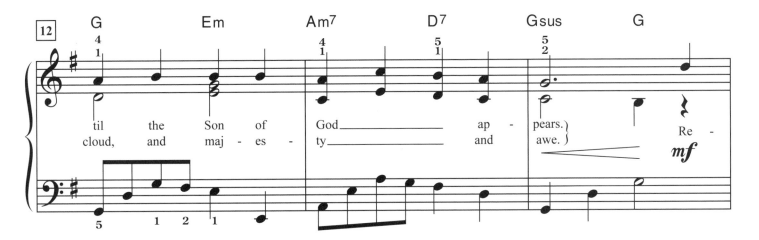

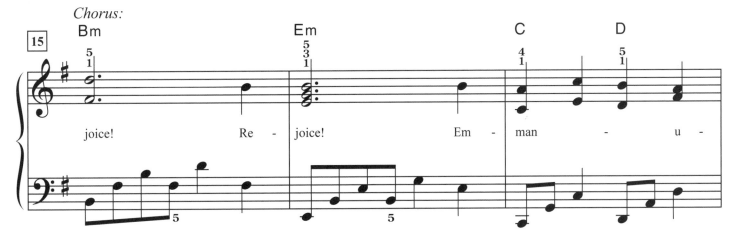

Chorus:

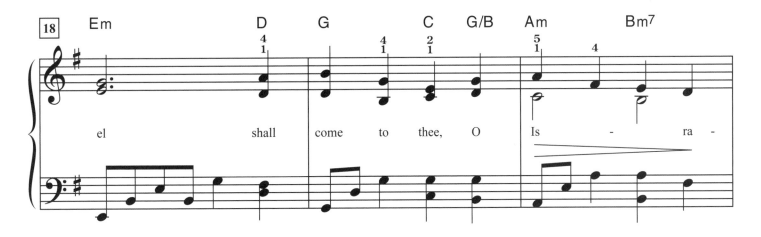

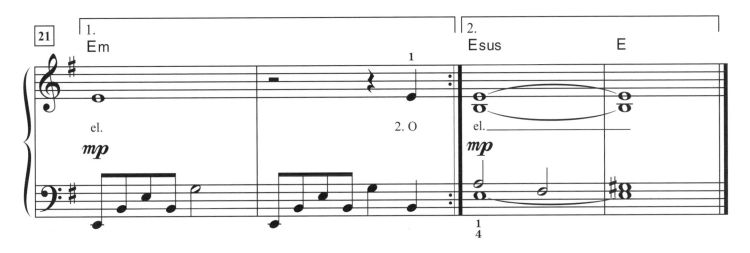

O Holy Night

Words and Music by
J. S. Dwight and Adolphe Adam
Arr. Dan Coates

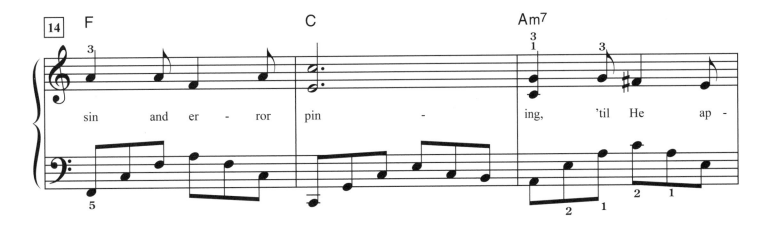

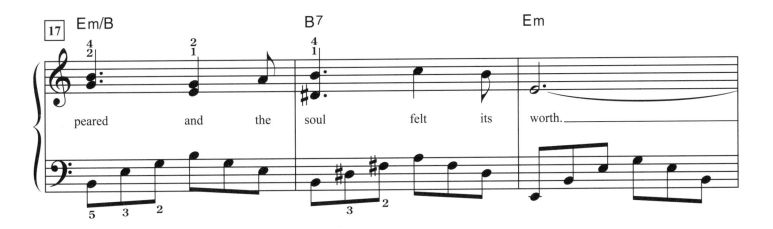

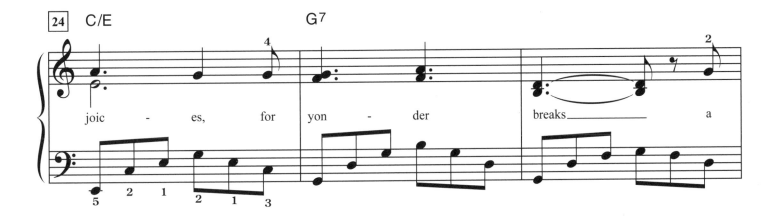

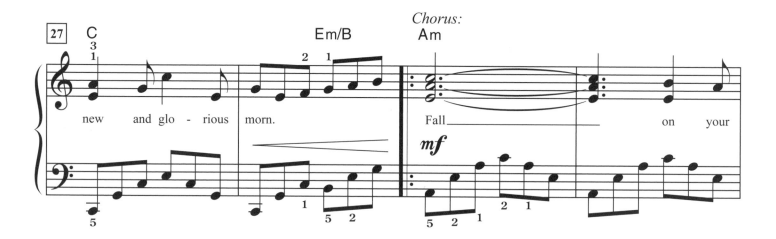

Chorus:

new and glo - rious morn. Fall_____ on your

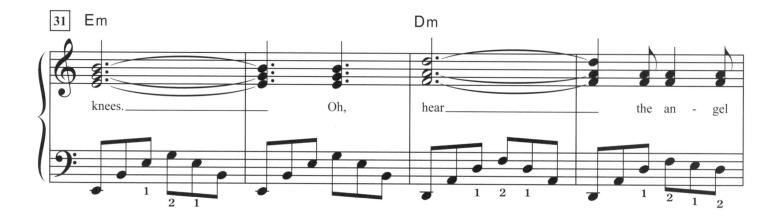

knees._____ Oh, hear_____ the an - gel

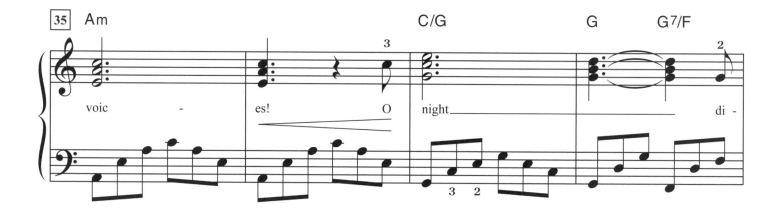

voic - es! O night_____ di-

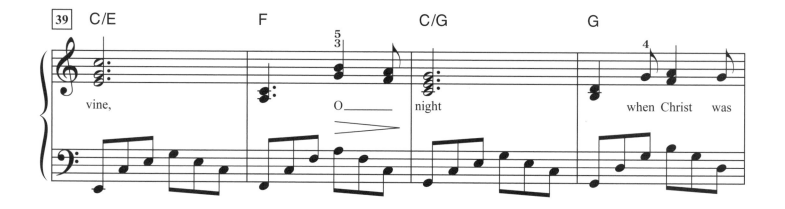

vine, O_____ night when Christ was

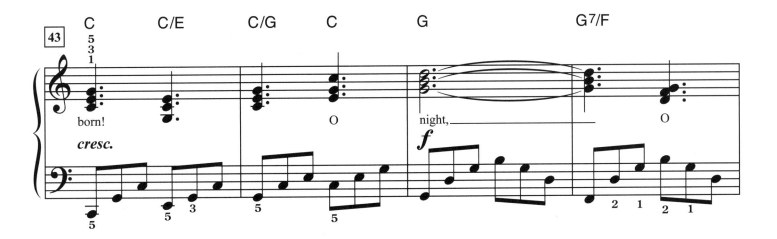

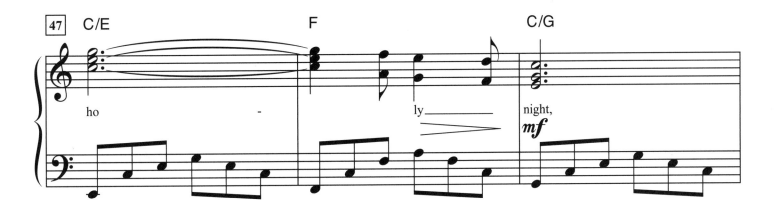

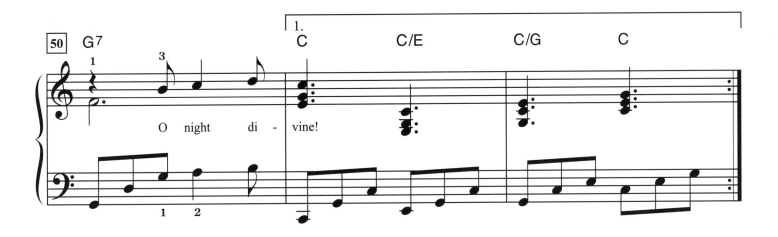

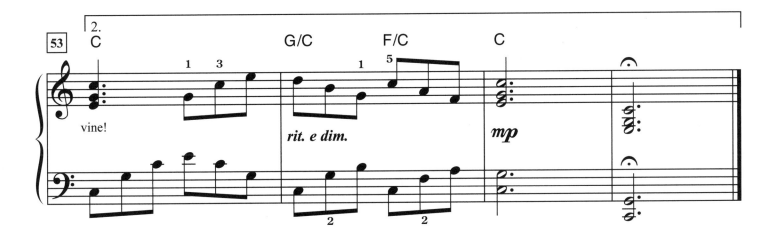

O Little Town of Bethlehem

Words by Phillips Brooks
Music by Lewis H. Redner
Arr. Dan Coates

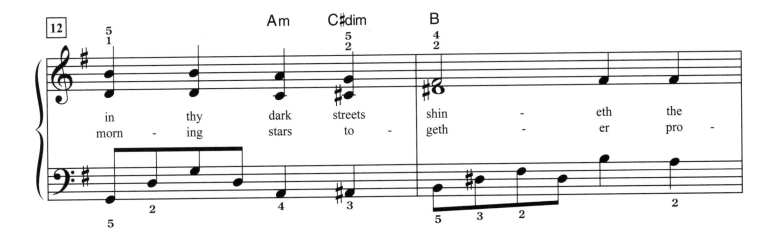

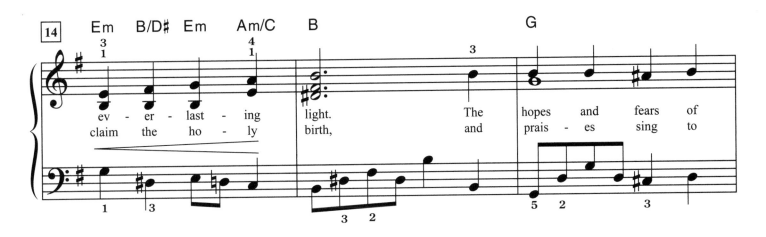

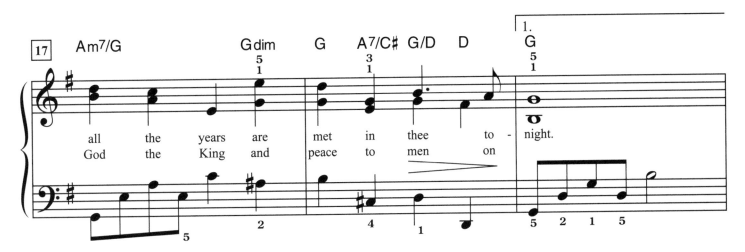

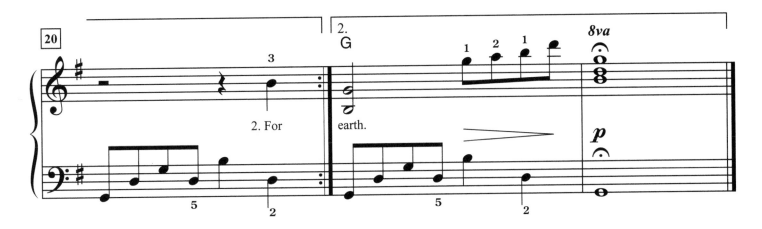

Rudolph, the Red-Nosed Reindeer

Words and Music by Johnny Marks
Arr. Dan Coates

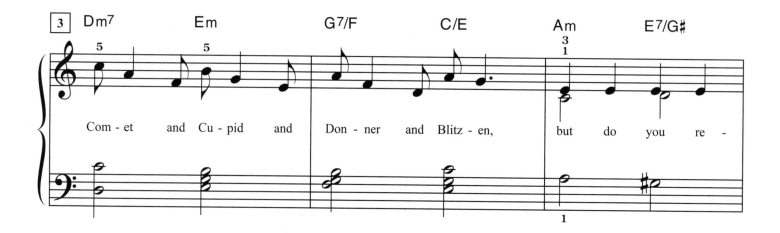

Chorus:

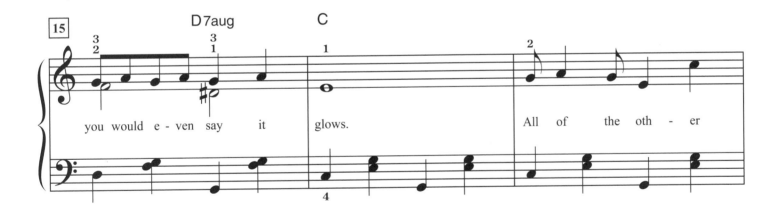

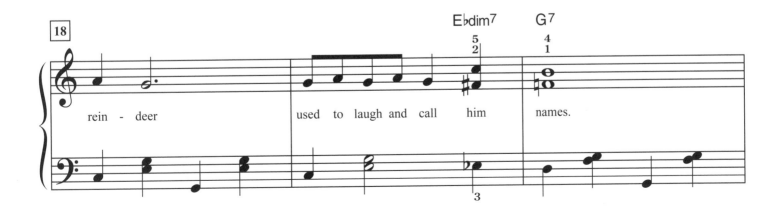

They nev - er let poor Ru - dolph join in an - y rein - deer

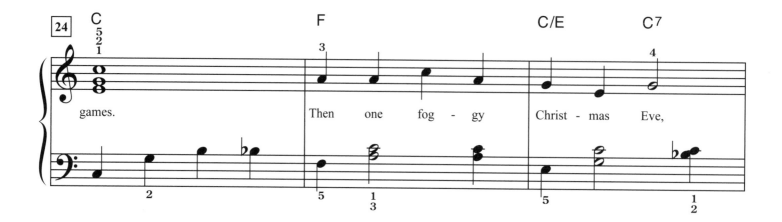

games. Then one fog - gy Christ - mas Eve,

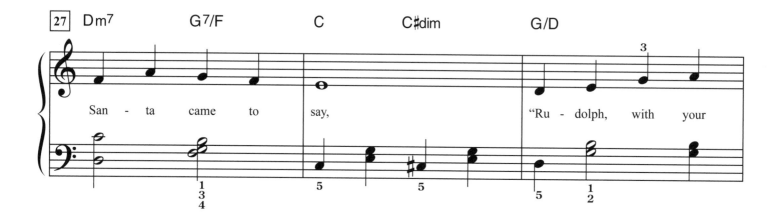

San - ta came to say, "Ru - dolph, with your

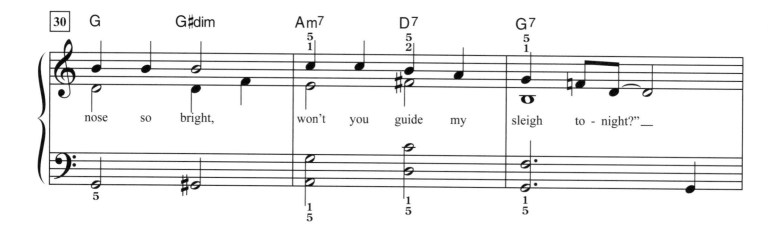

nose so bright, won't you guide my sleigh to - night?"

Then how   the   rein - deer   loved   him,   as they shout - ed out   with

glee: "Ru - dolph   the   red - nosed   rein - deer,

you'll go down in his - to - ry!"   you'll   go   down   in

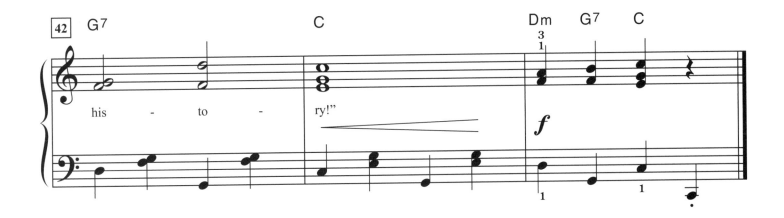

his - to - ry!"

Santa Claus Is Comin' to Town

Words by Haven Gillespie
Music by J. Fred Coots
Arr. Dan Coates

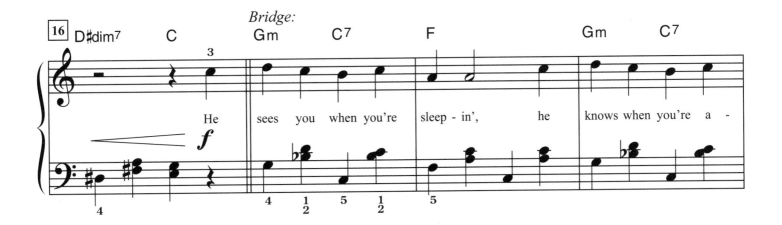

Bridge:

16 D#dim7　　C　　Gm　　C7　　F　　Gm　　C7

He sees you when you're sleep - in', he knows when you're a -

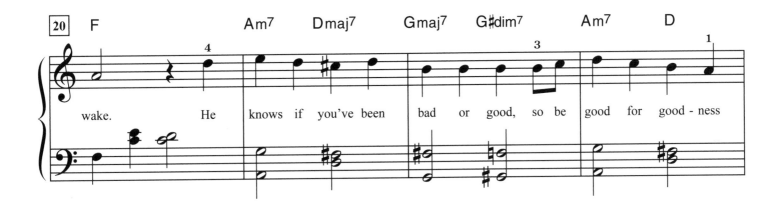

20 F　　Am7　Dmaj7　Gmaj7　G#dim7　Am7　D

wake. He knows if you've been bad or good, so be good for good - ness

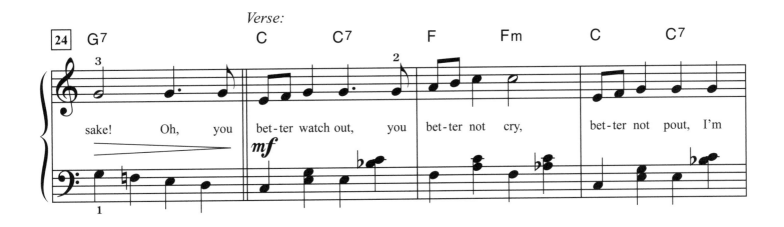

Verse:

24 G7　　C　　C7　　F　Fm　　C　　C7

sake! Oh, you bet-ter watch out, you bet-ter not cry, bet-ter not pout, I'm

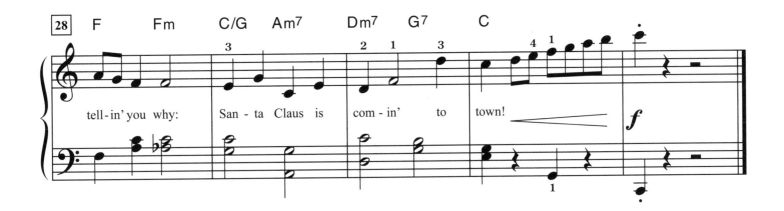

28 F　Fm　C/G　Am7　Dm7　G7　　C

tell-in' you why: San - ta Claus is com - in' to town!

Pat-a-pan

Words and Music by
Bernard De La Monnoye
Arr. Dan Coates

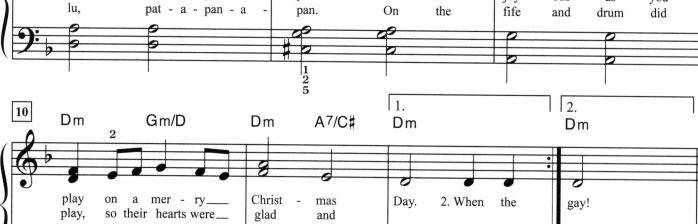

Rockin' Around the Christmas Tree

Words and Music by Johnny Marks
Arr. Dan Coates

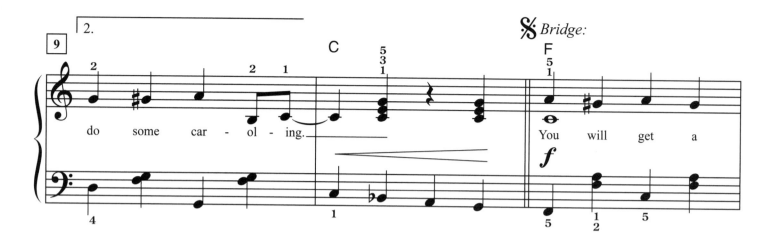

do some car - ol - ing. You will get a

sen - ti - men - tal feel - ing when you hear

voic - es sing - ing, "Let's be jol - ly! Deck the halls with

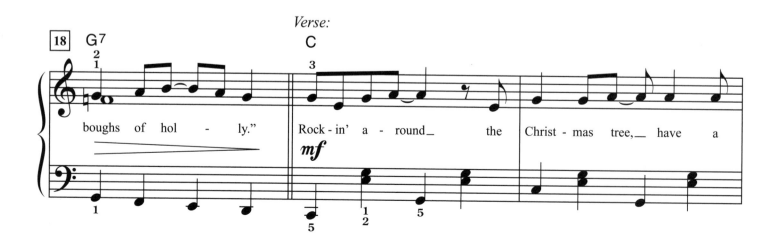

boughs of hol - ly." Rock - in' a - round the Christ - mas tree, have a

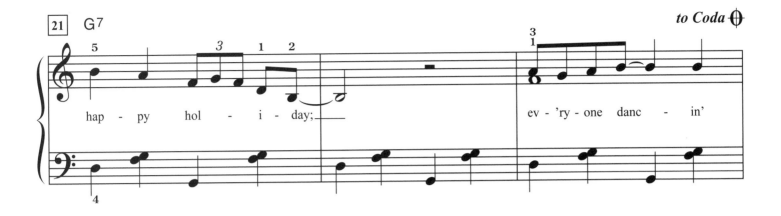

to Coda

hap - py hol - i - day; ____ ev - 'ry - one danc - in'

D.S. al Coda

mer - ri - ly ___ in the new old fash - ioned way.

Coda

mer - ri - ly ___ in the new old fash - ioned ___

cresc.

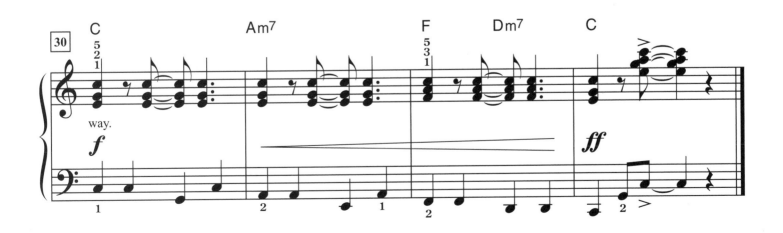

way.

f

ff

Santa Baby

Words and Music by Joan Javits, Philip Springer
and Tony Springer
Arr. Dan Coates

Moderately slow

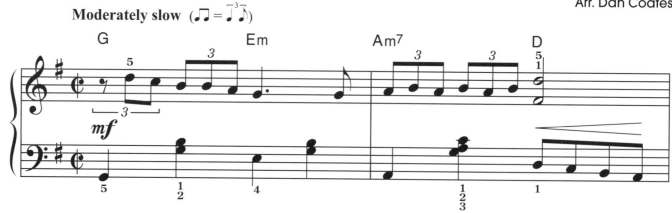

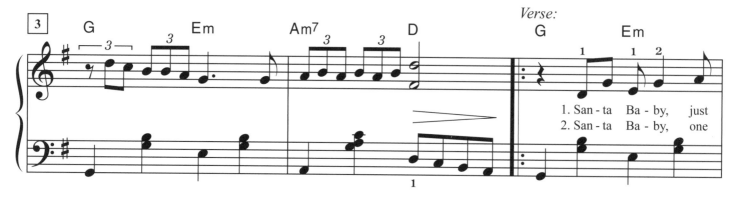

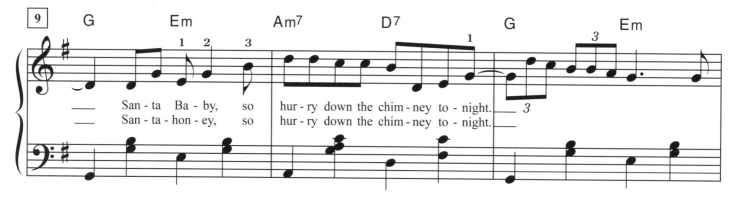

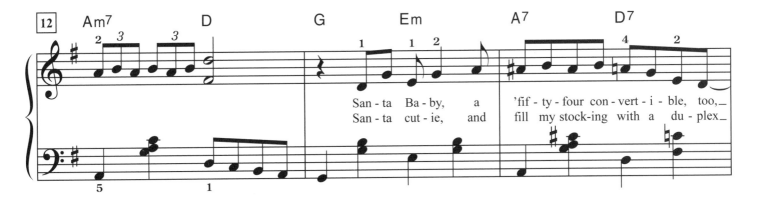

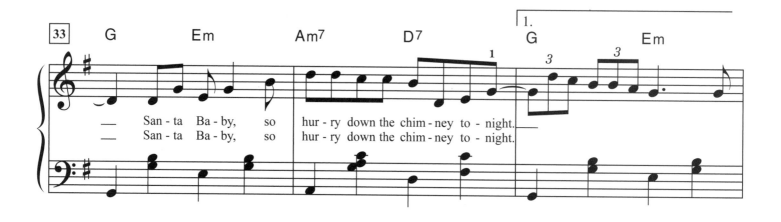

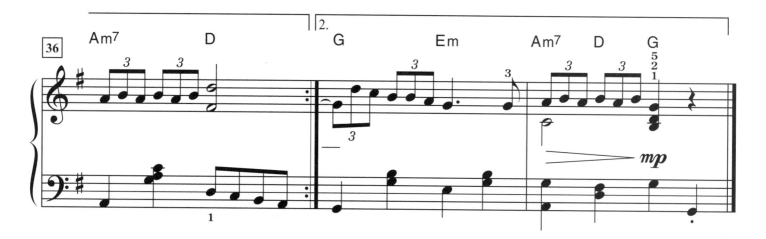

Silent Night

Words and Music by
Joseph Mohr and Franz Gruber
Arr. Dan Coates

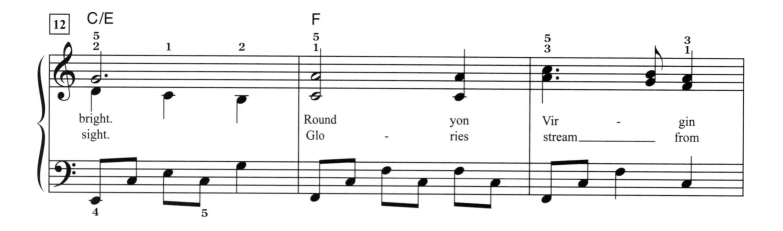

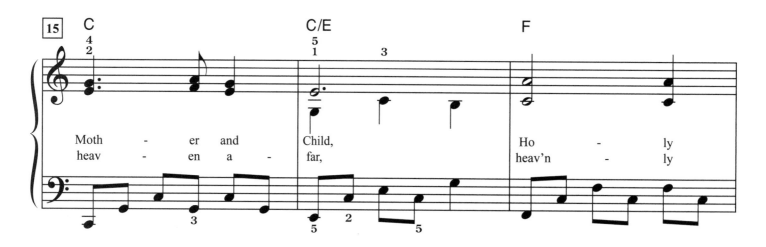

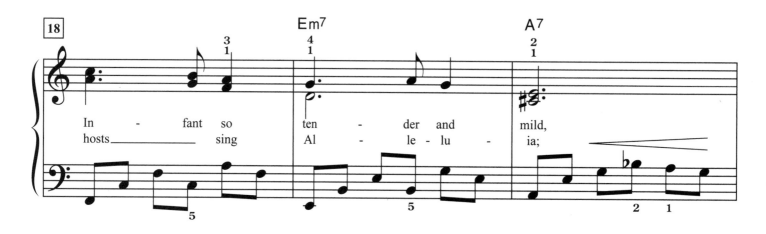

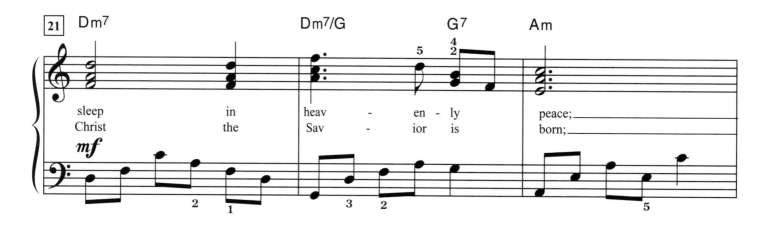

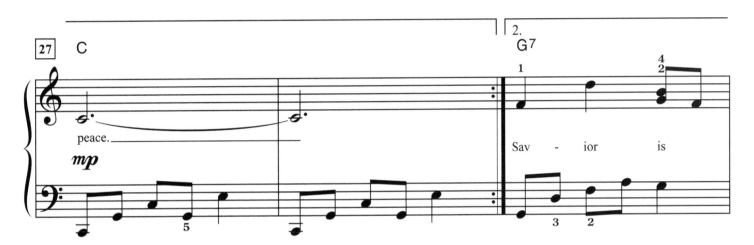

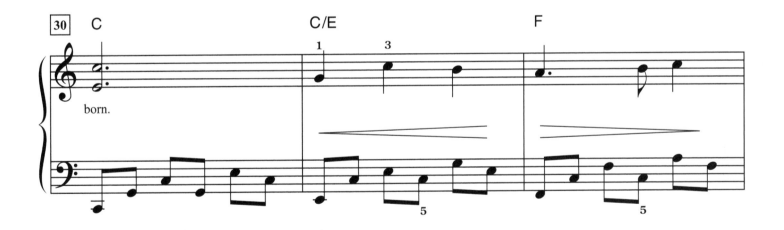

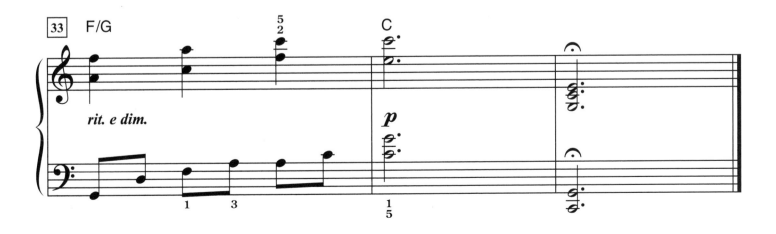

Sleigh Ride

Music by Leroy Anderson
Words by Mitchell Parish
Arr. Dan Coates

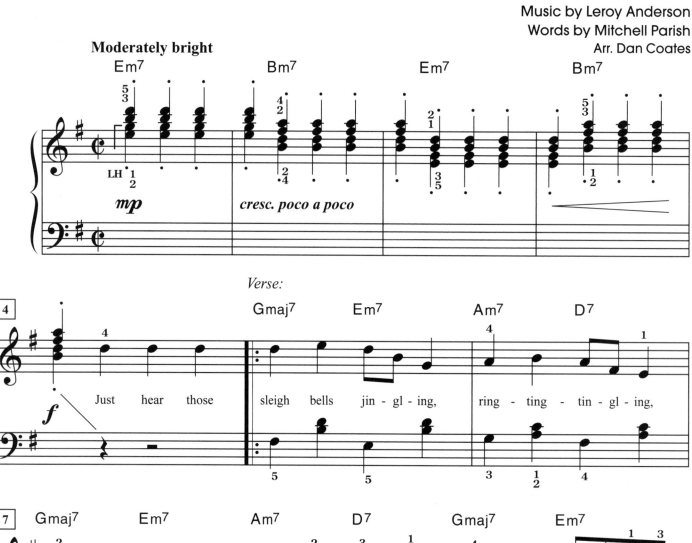

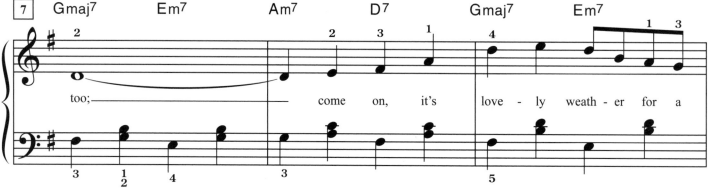

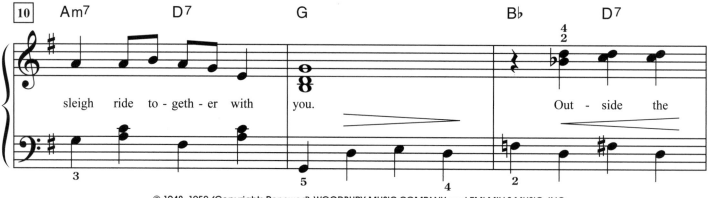

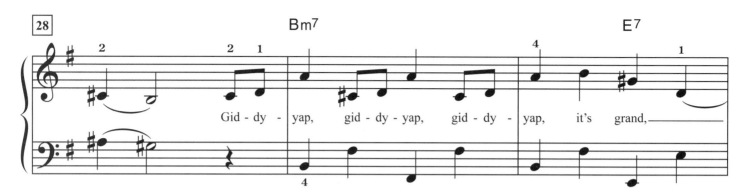

Gid-dy - yap, gid-dy-yap, gid-dy - yap, it's grand,____

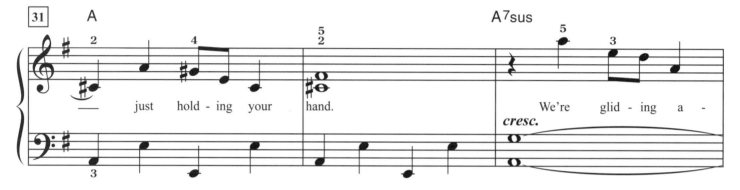

____ just hold-ing your hand. We're glid-ing a -

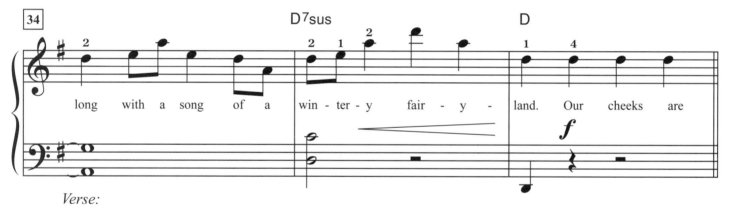

long with a song of a win-ter-y fair-y - land. Our cheeks are

Verse:

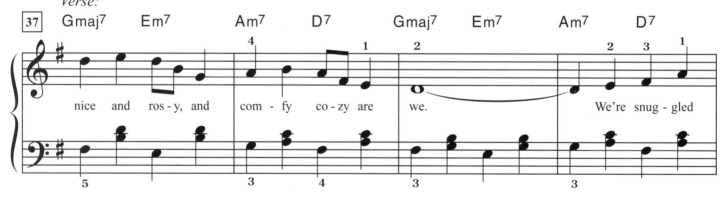

nice and ros-y, and com-fy co-zy are we. We're snug-gled

up to-geth-er like two birds of a feath-er would be.

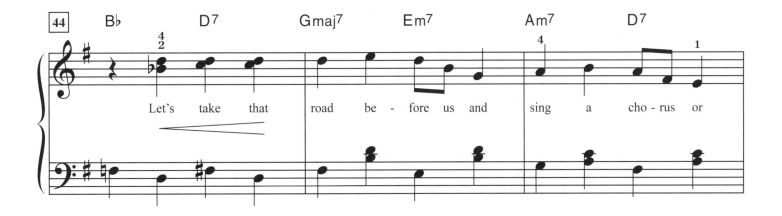

44

Bb   D7   Gmaj7   Em7   Am7   D7

Let's take that road be - fore us and sing a cho - rus or

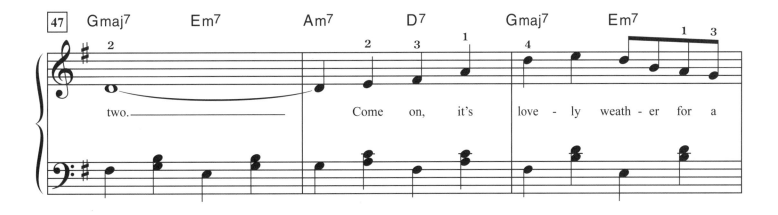

47

Gmaj7   Em7   Am7   D7   Gmaj7   Em7

two._____ Come on, it's love - ly weath - er for a

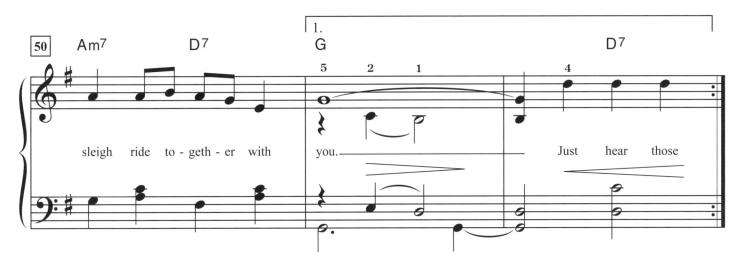

50

Am7   D7   G   D7

1.

sleigh ride to - geth - er with you._____ Just hear those

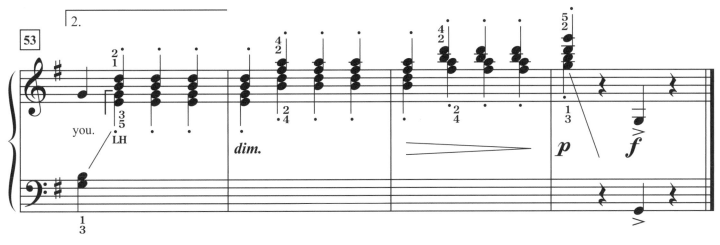

53

2.

you.

dim.   p   f

These Are the Special Times

Words and Music by Diane Warren
Arr. Dan Coates

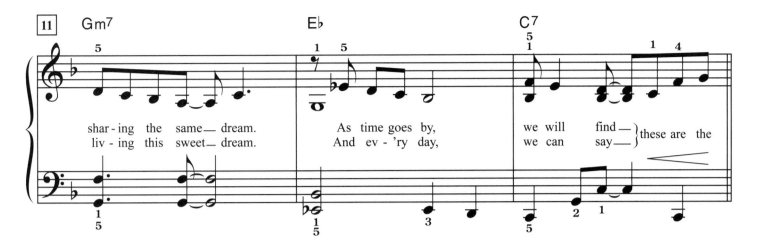

11 Gm7   E♭   C7

shar-ing the same— dream.   As time goes by,   we will find— } these are the
liv-ing this sweet— dream.   And ev-'ry day,   we can say—

Chorus:

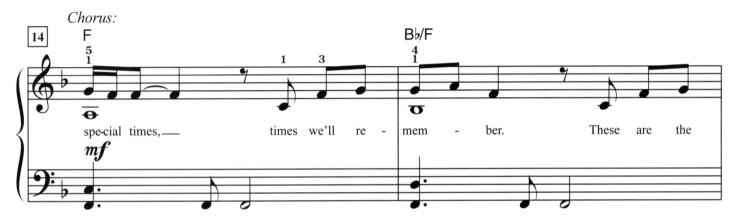

14 F   B♭/F

spe-cial times,—   times we'll re-mem - ber.   These are the

mf

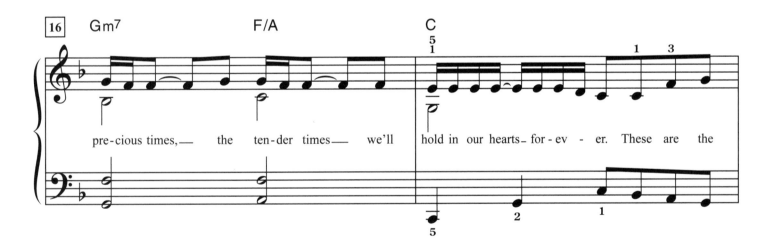

16 Gm7   F/A   C

pre-cious times,— the ten-der times— we'll   hold in our hearts— for-ev - er. These are the

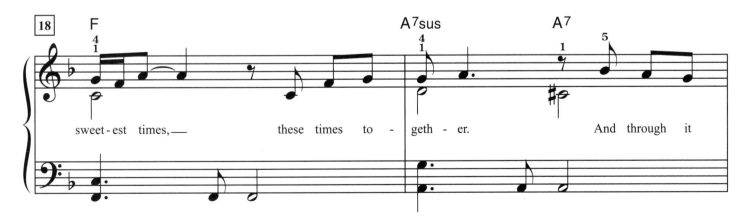

18 F   A7sus   A7

sweet-est times,—   these times to - geth - er.   And through it

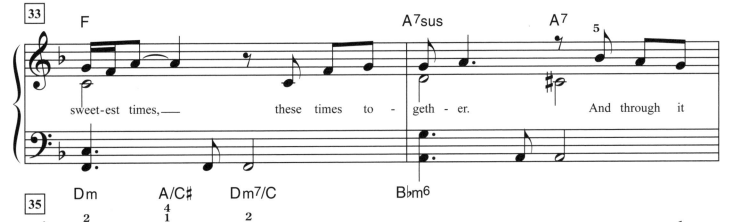

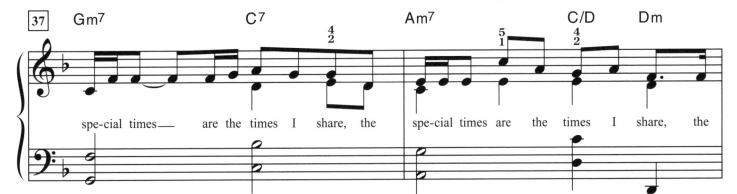

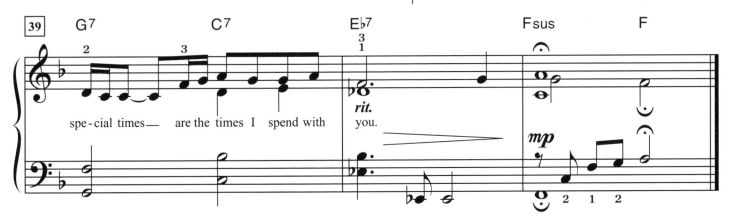

Toyland

Words by Glen MacDonough
Music by Victor Herbert
Arr. Dan Coates

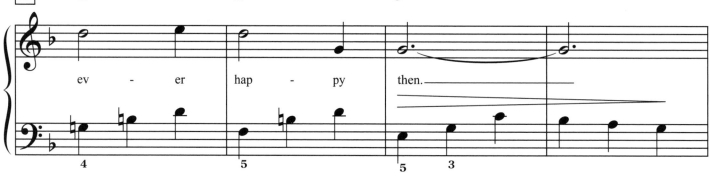

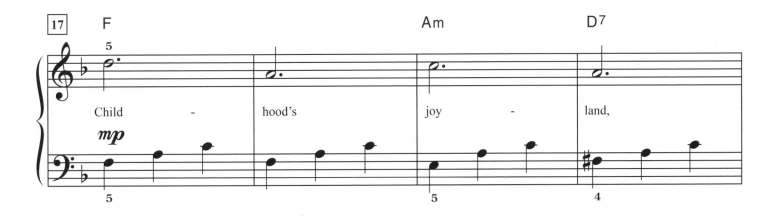

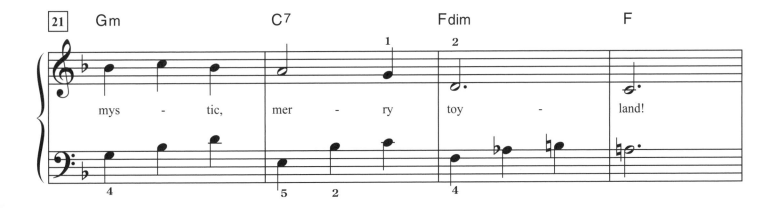

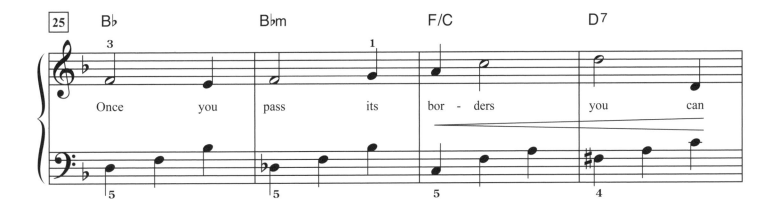

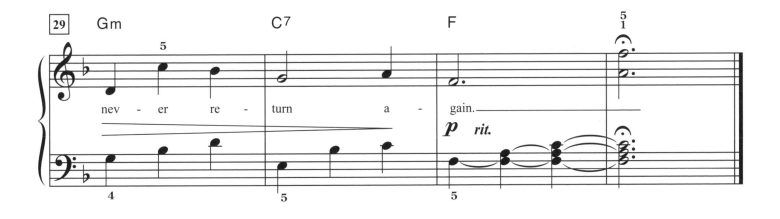

The Twelve Days of Christmas

Traditional English carol
Arr. Dan Coates

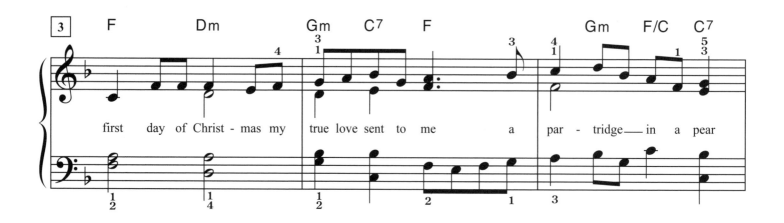

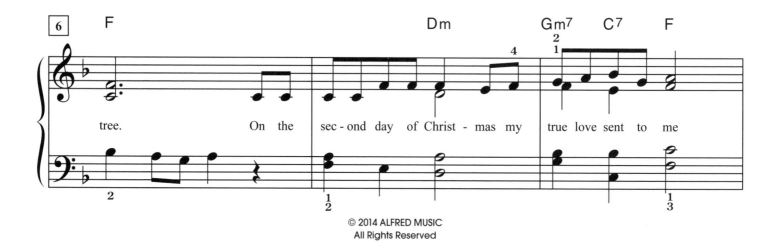

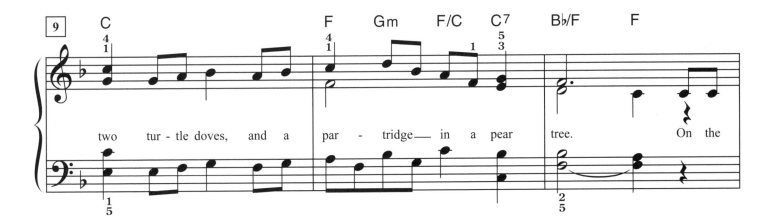

two tur - tle doves, and a par - tridge— in a pear tree. On the

third day of Christ - mas my true love sent to me three French— hens,

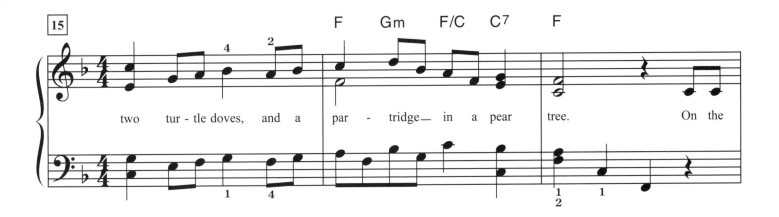

two tur - tle doves, and a par - tridge— in a pear tree. On the

fourth day of Christ - mas my true love sent to me four call - ing birds, three French— hens,

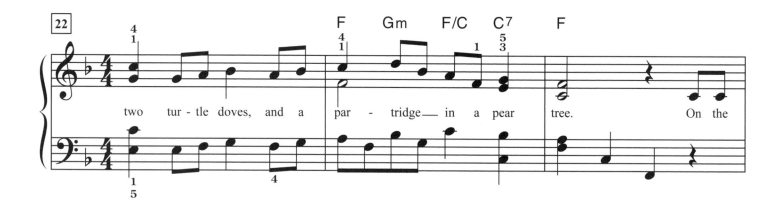

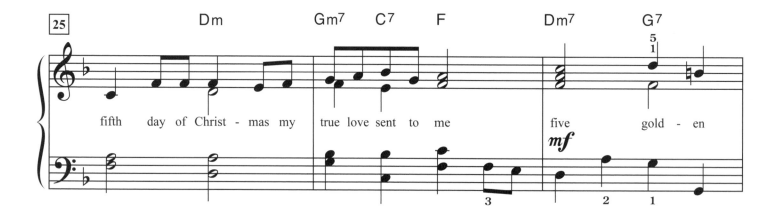

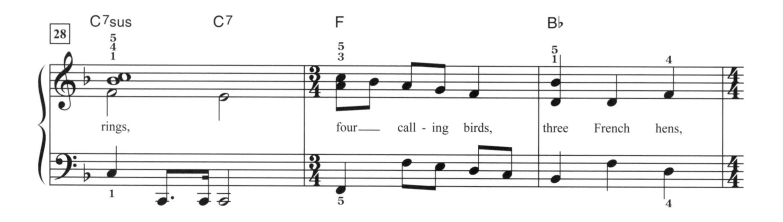

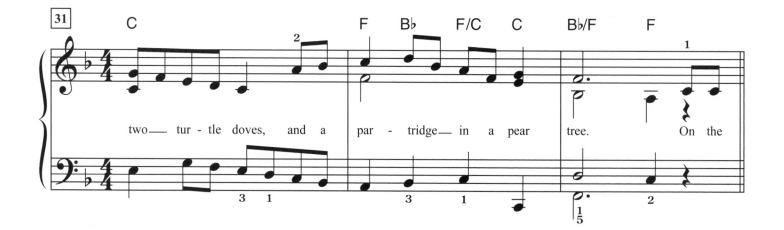

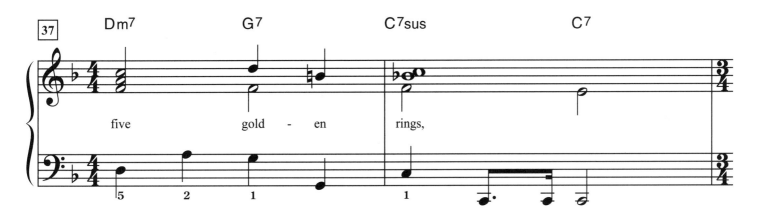

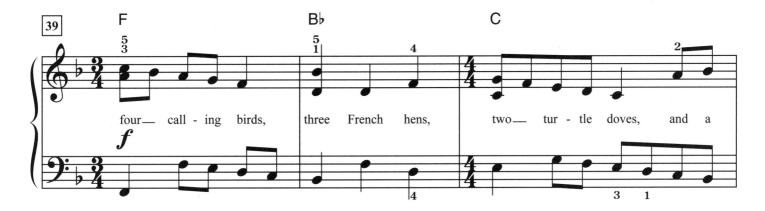

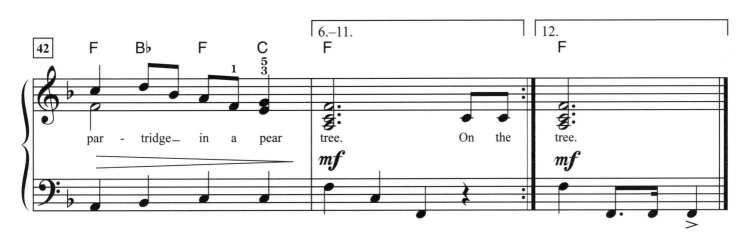

Ukrainian Bell Carol

Mykola Leontovych
Arr. Dan Coates

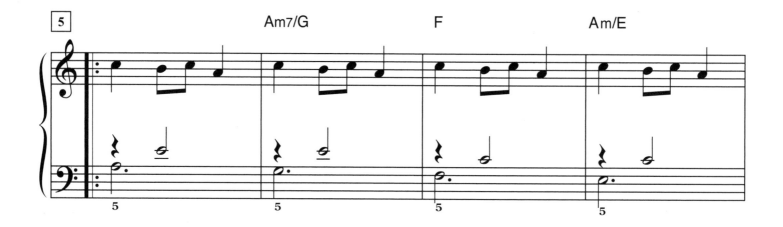

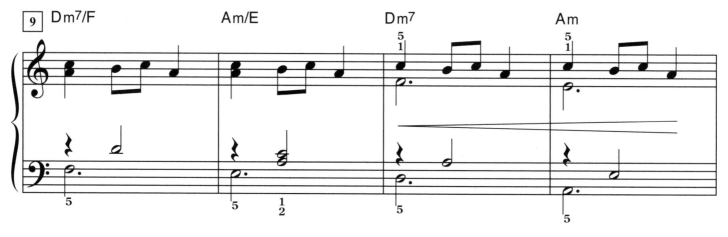

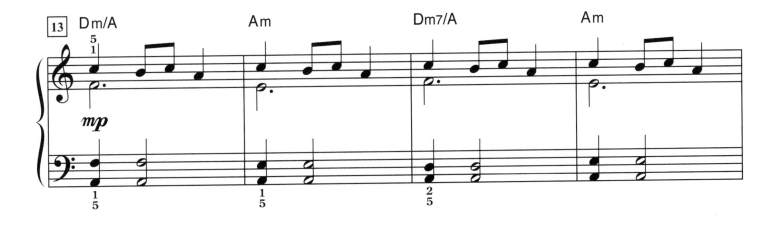

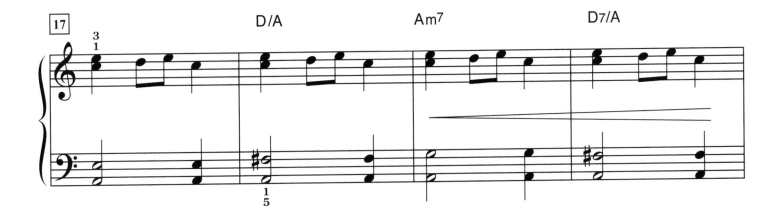

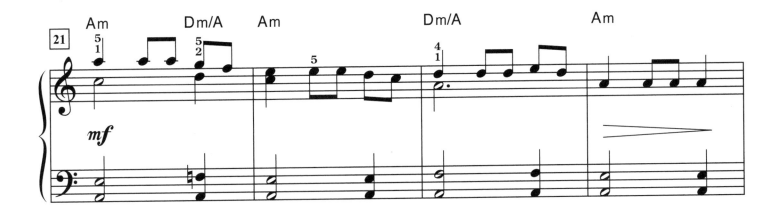

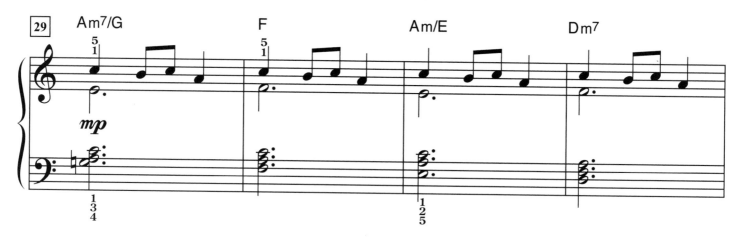

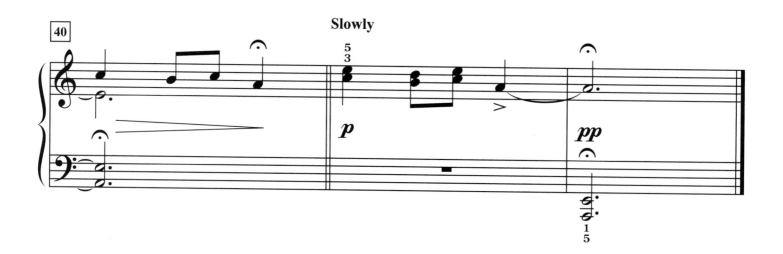

Up on the Housetop

Words and Music by
Benjamin R. Hanby
Arr. Dan Coates

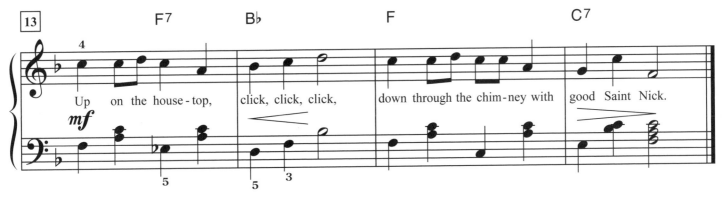

We Wish You a Merry Christmas

Traditional English carol
Arr. Dan Coates

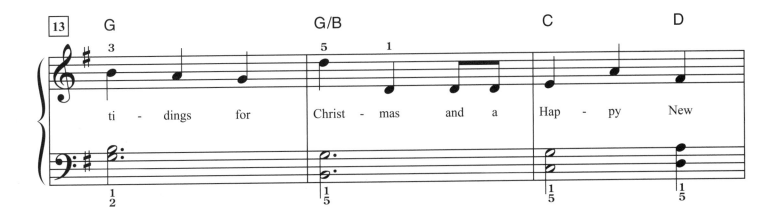

Chorus:

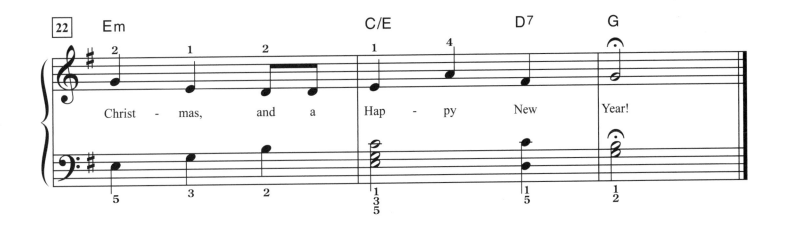

What Child Is This?

Words by William C. Dix
Traditional English melody
Arr. Dan Coates

Moderately slow

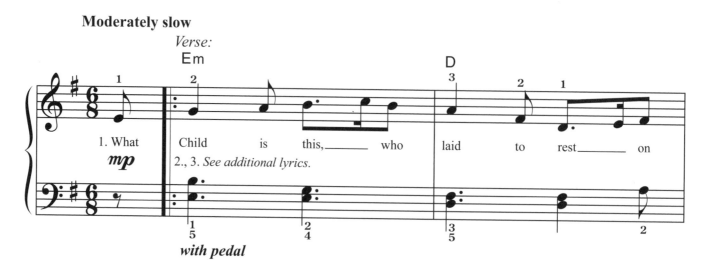

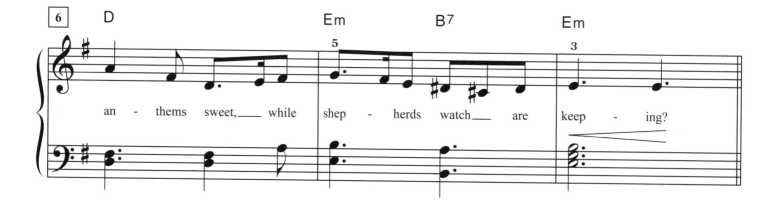

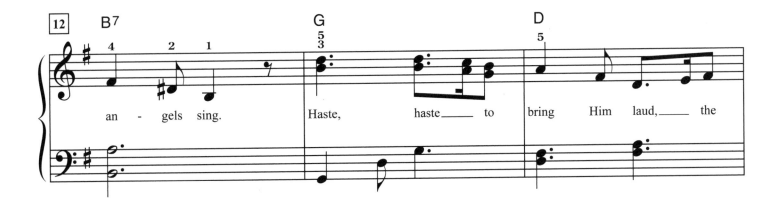

Verse 2:
Why lies He in such mean estate,
Where ox and ass are feeding?
Good Christian fear, for sinners here
The silent word is pleading.
Nails, spear shall pierce Him through;
The Cross be born for me, for you,
Hail, hail the word made flesh,
The Babe, the Son of Mary.

Verse 3:
So bring Him incense, gold and myrrh,
Come peasant, king to own Him.
The King of Kings salvation brings;
Let loving hearts enthrone Him.
Raise, raise the song on high
The Virgin sings her lullaby;
Joy, joy for Christ is born.
The Babe, the Son of Mary.

We Three Kings of Orient Are

Words and Music by John H. Hopkins
Arr. Dan Coates

153

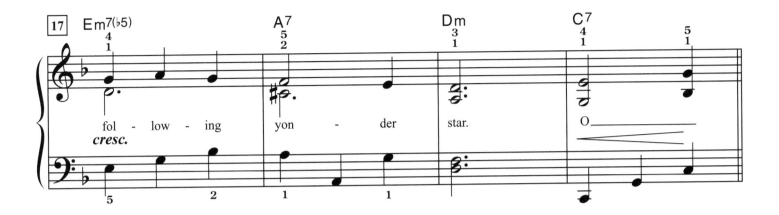

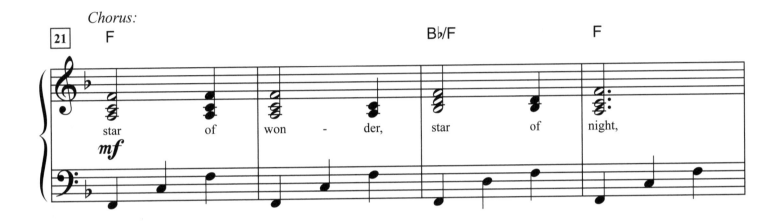

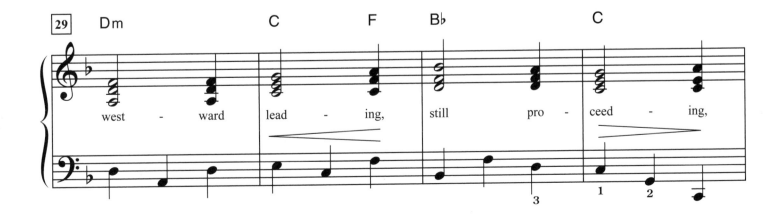

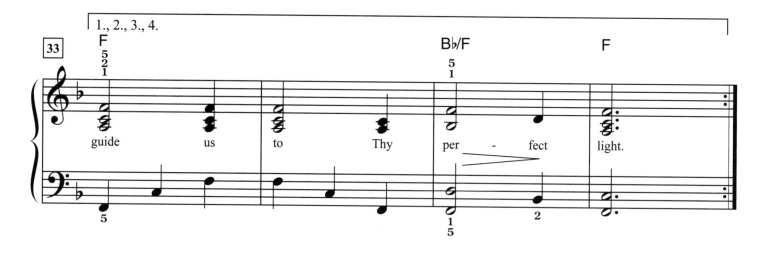

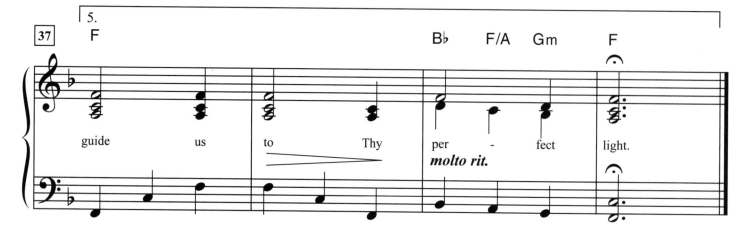

Verse 2:
Born a King on Bethlehem's plain,
Gold I bring, to crown Him again,
King forever, ceasing never
Over us all to reign.
(To Chorus:)

Verse 3:
Frankincense to offer have I,
Incense owns a Deity nigh.
Prayer and praising, all men raising
Worship Him, God most high.
(To Chorus:)

Verse 4:
Myrrh is mine, its bitter perfume
Breathes a life of gathering gloom;
Sorrowing, sighing, bleeding, dying,
Sealed in the stone-cold tomb.
(To Chorus:)

Verse 5:
Glorious now behold Him arise,
King and God and sacrifice.
Alleluia, Alleluia,
Earth to heaven replies.
(To Chorus:)

When Christmas Comes to Town
(from *The Polar Express*)

Words and Music by
Alan Silvestri and Glen Ballard
Arr. Dan Coates

156

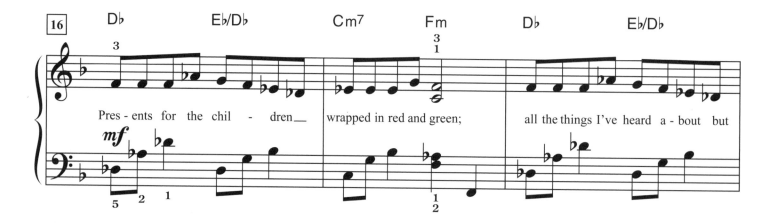

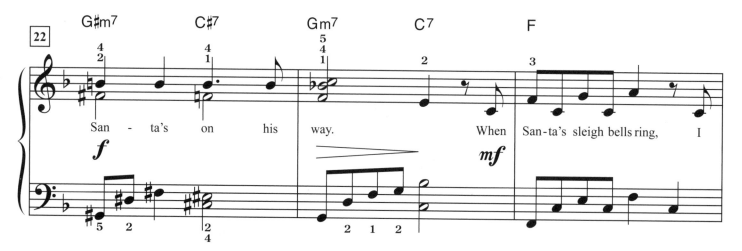

lis- ten all a - round. The her - ald an - gels sing; I nev - er hear a sound. And

Gm7   C   F   B♭   F/A   Gm7   C7

all the dreams of chil - dren, once lost, will all be found. That's all I want when Christ-mas comes to

Dm7   G7   Gm7   C7   *a tempo*

town.   That's all I want when Christ-mas comes to town.

rit.

mp

molto rit.   *p*

You're a Mean One, Mr. Grinch

(from *How the Grinch Stole Christmas*)

Music by Albert Hague
Lyrics by Dr. Seuss
Arr. Dan Coates

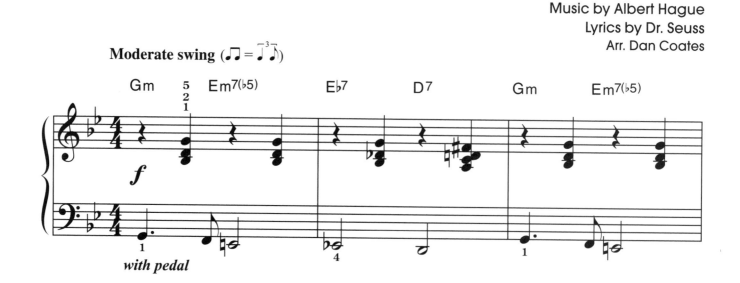

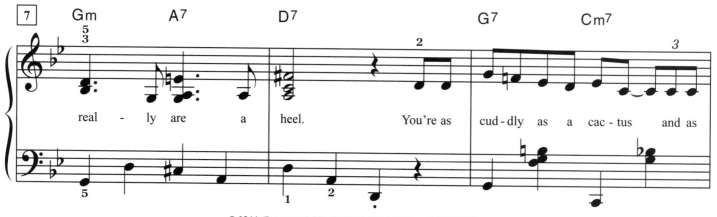

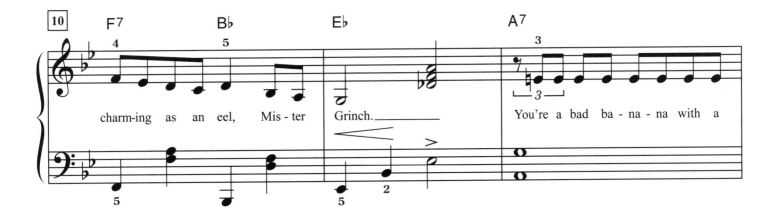

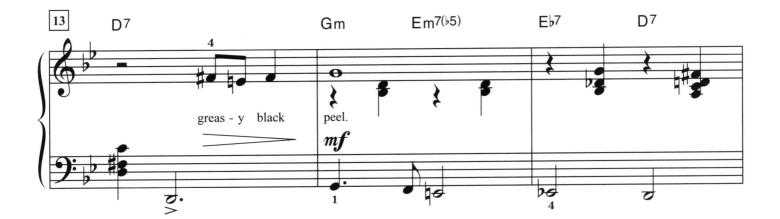

brain is full of spi-ders, you got gar-lic_____ in your soul, Mis-ter Grinch._____

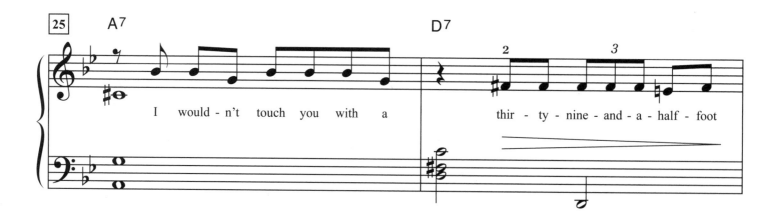

I would-n't touch you with a thir-ty-nine-and-a-half-foot

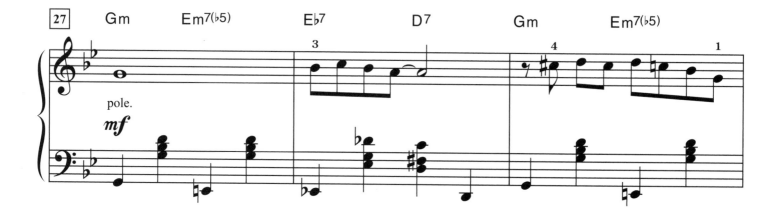

pole.

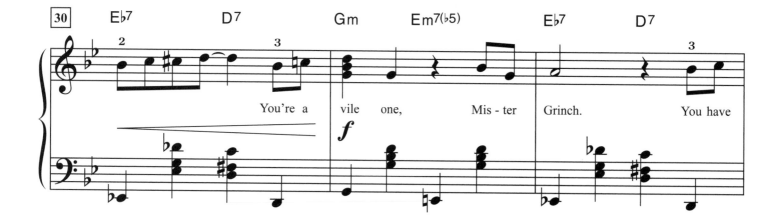

You're a vile one, Mis-ter Grinch. You have

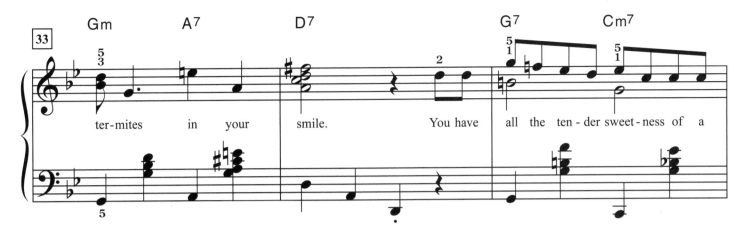

ter-mites in your smile. You have all the ten-der sweet-ness of a

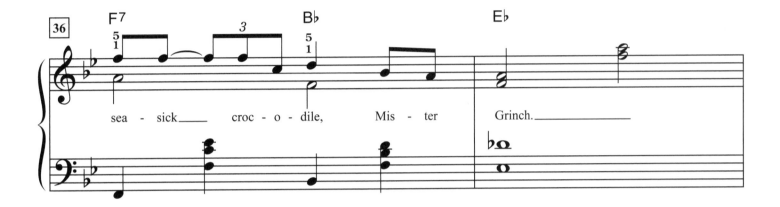

sea - sick_____ croc - o - dile, Mis - ter Grinch._____

Giv - en the choice be - tween you, I'd take the sea - sick croc - o -

dile.

Winter Wonderland

Words by Dick Smith
Music by Felix Bernard
Arr. Dan Coates

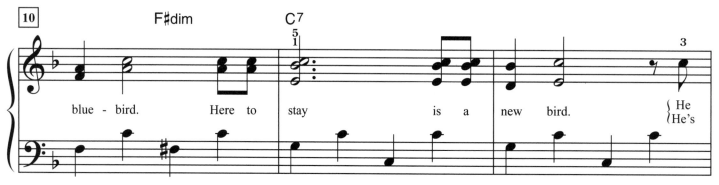

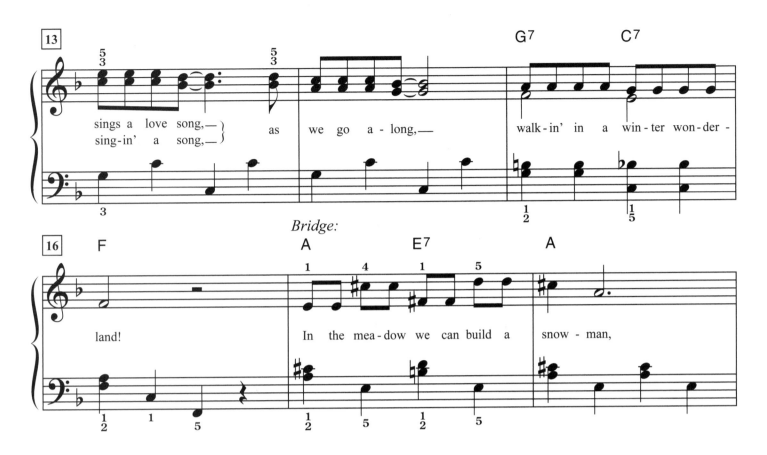

Bridge:

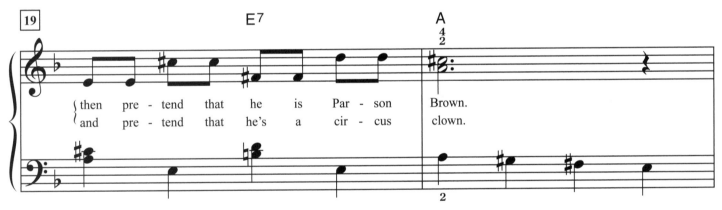

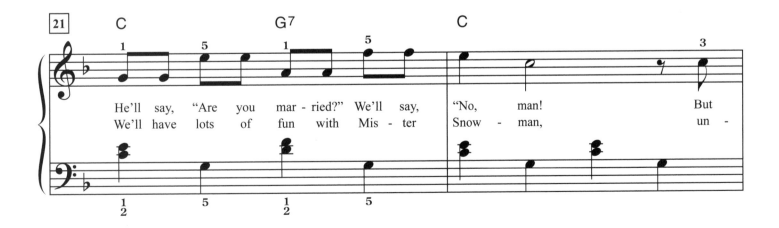

23

D7/F#   **G7/F**   **C7/E**

you can do the job when you're in town!"   Lat - er
til the oth - er kid - dies knock 'im down!   When it

Verse:

25

F   **F#dim**   **C7**

on,   we'll con - spire,—   as we dream   by the
snows,   ain't it thrill - in',   though your nose   gets a

f

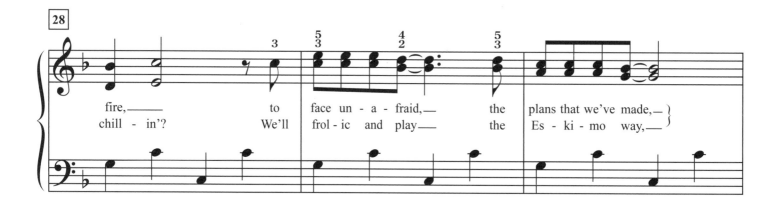

28

fire,—   to   face un - a - fraid,—   the   plans that we've made,—
chill - in'?   We'll   frol - ic and play   the   Es - ki - mo way,—

31

G7   **C7**   1. **F**   2. **F**

walk - in' in a win - ter won - der - land!   Sleigh bells   land!

mf

'Zat You, Santa Claus?

Words and Music by Jack Fox
Arr. Dan Coates

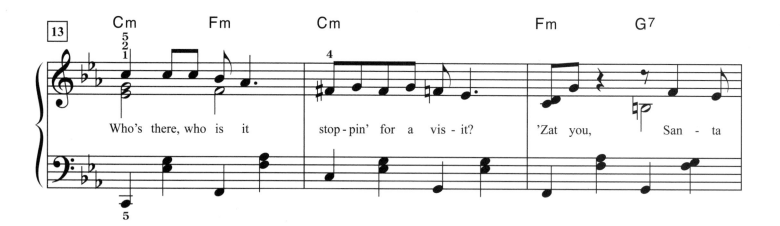

Who's there, who is it stop-pin' for a vis-it? 'Zat you, San-ta

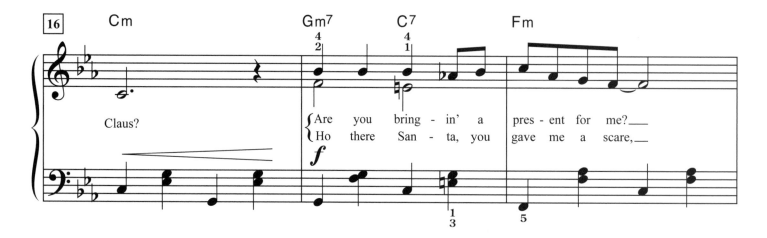

Claus?

Are you bring-in' a pres-ent for me?___
Ho there San-ta, you gave me a scare,___

Some-thin' pleas-ant-ly pleas-ant for me?___ But it's just what I've
Now stop teas-in' 'cause I know you're there._ We don't b'lieve in no

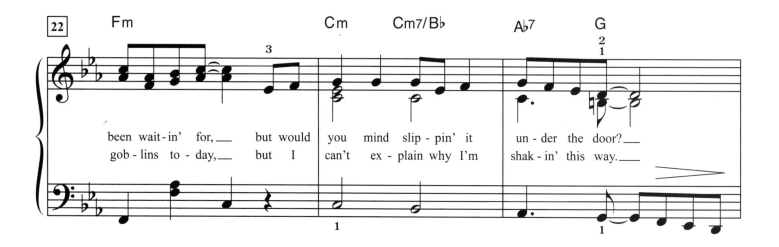

been wait-in' for,___ but would you mind slip-pin' it un-der the door?___
gob-lins to-day,___ but I can't ex-plain why I'm shak-in' this way.___

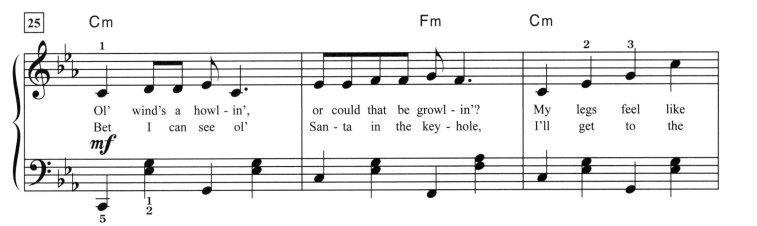

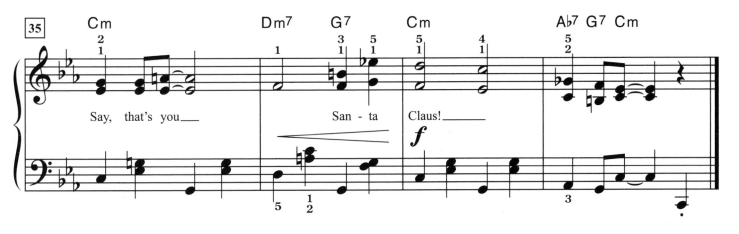